WHEN
GOOD
ENOUGH
IS NOT
ENOUGH

WHEN GOOD ENOUGH IS NOT ENOUGH

PURSUING THE PROMISED LIFE

ALLAN LOCKERMAN

Book Editor: Wanda Griffith
Editorial Assistant: Tammy Hatfield
Copy Editors: Oreeda Burnette
Esther Metaxas
Cresta Shawver

Library of Congress Catalog Card Number: 2003112315
ISBN: 0-87148-131-6
Copyright © 2003 by Pathway Press
Cleveland, Tennessee 37311
All Rights Reserved
Printed in the United States of America

Dedicated to

ALICE, ROB, KELLI, JEFF AND JENNIFER,

who make my life more than mere experience.

Table of Contents

Preface

For I know the thoughts that I think toward you, says the Lord, thoughts of peace and not of evil, to give you a future and a hope (Jeremiah 29:11).

The young man asking the question was a member of my congregation. "What do you consider to be the most challenging task you face as you lead our church?" I was trying to be careful with my response. It was not that I didn't have an answer. I wasn't sure the young man would grasp what I was going to say. After 30 years in the pastorate, serving congregations as small as 17 members to as large as 7,000, I knew the challenge well. Simply stated, how do you convince people that "good enough" is not enough?

There is a sin that threatens to rob us of our effectiveness and diminish the attraction of our faith—a sin that disqualifies many as witnesses for Christ. Surely, this is not news to anyone. However, what might be surprising is what this sin is. It does not get a lot of attention. Few have heard of it. It is subtle and not easy to spot, but it is found in every corner of the Kingdom. It is not moral or even theological in nature, though it has moral and theological implications.

So what is this sin? It could be called the sin of "settling." Most have been guilty of it—I have. It is not just falling short; rather, it is falling short and growing comfortable. I sometimes refer to this as the "good-enough syndrome." It isn't unique to Christians, but it is especially distasteful when it gets into the faith. The evidence of this malady can be found in statements such as these:

- I wouldn't describe my spiritual life as deep, but I guess it's good enough.

- My life hasn't been what I had hoped, but I can't complain; it's good enough.

- I don't pray as I should, but I think my prayer life is good enough.

- Our marriage isn't what we would like, but I guess it is good enough.

Question: When did "good enough" become enough? What ever happened to the concept of excellence? Shouldn't God's people want the best that God has for them? Shouldn't we claim what is rightfully ours? Shouldn't we pursue the promised life? Indeed, we should!

The Old Testament Book of Joshua tells of people like us, who spent the better part of their lives settling for less, until one day "good enough" was not enough. Under the leadership of Joshua, they claimed the land and life God had promised. There are many parallels between these ancient Hebrews and believers today. The story is familiar. Written nearly 1,400 years before the time of Christ, it is as relevant today as the day it was penned. However, it is often misunderstood and misapplied. Some think of the Book of Joshua as an analogy of the believer's quest of heaven. Many believe it promises a better life by and by. This picture has been nurtured over the years by the sentimental words of some of our most beloved hymns:

"We're marching to Zion."

"I am bound for the Promised Land."

The songwriters imply that the land of Canaan, Beulah Land and the Promised Land are types of heaven itself.

The following verse from the old favorite hymn draws the picture vividly:

> On Jordan's stormy banks I stand
> And cast a wishful eye
> To Canaan's fair and happy land,
> Where my possessions lie.

This is a beautiful hymn, but we shouldn't build our theology around it. "Canaan's fair and happy land" is not heaven; it is the life we are to live here and now. The Book of Joshua is the historical counterpart to Ephesians in the New Testament. It pictures victory in Christian life and illustrates how God's people can claim what is rightfully theirs.

Joshua in the Old Testament and Ephesians in the New Testament point believers to a better life than most are living—not a life to come after we die, but a full and meaningful life now. Jesus said, "I have come that [you] may have life, and that [you] may have it more abundantly" (John 10:10).

The Book of Joshua will form the backdrop for the pages ahead. We will journey with Joshua as he leads these ancient Hebrews across the Jordan into Canaan. We will learn timeless truths about the life of promise. The Book of Joshua shows us clearly that God does not want His children to settle for less; He wants us to claim what is rightfully ours.

The great challenge of leadership in the 21st-century church may well be the challenge of moving Christians beyond "good enough." In a world that demands and expects quality, why would anyone want to join the average church? More importantly, why would anyone want to follow Christ when those who claim to follow Him settle for so little? If we are to be vibrant witnesses for Christ, "good enough" will *not* be enough!

There is a promised life . . . a life that fits your unique gifts and personality . . . a life that is dynamic and evolving . . . a life that matters now and for eternity. Is there a formula that will produce such a life? No, but there is a secret that people who live the life of promise have discovered: God meets us at the point of our desire. In fact, He promises to give us the desires of our hearts. The question is, Do we want more or have we settled? Perhaps the task of convincing people that "good enough is not enough" is our second most challenging task. The first may be to convince ourselves.

Introduction

Now all these things happened to them as examples, and they were written for our admonition, upon whom the ends of the ages have come (1 Corinthians 10:11).

I am a student of the Old Testament. Please notice I said *student*, not scholar. I do not claim to be an expert, but I am certainly more than a fan of these wonderful and unusual stories.

I come from a faith tradition that puts a high value on the Scripture. We are fond of pounding the pulpit and waxing eloquent about the inerrant and infallible Word of God. I certainly have no argument with this. However, I do find it interesting that many people who take this stand ignore so much of the Word. Many seem to regard the Old Testament as a prelude to the Scripture. Some would argue that Christians are New Testament people. Nonsense! As Christians, we are people of the Bible, the whole book, Old and New Testament alike. We forget that when Jesus spoke directly of the Scriptures, He was referring to the Old Testament. For that matter, the same was true for Paul, Peter, Jude and John, because the New Testament had not been written.

Though Jesus probably intended to include the New Testament when He said, "Till heaven and earth pass away, one jot or one tittle will by no means pass from the law till all is fulfilled" (Matthew 5:18), it was the Old Testament of which He spoke. When Paul said, "All Scripture is given by inspiration of God" (2 Timothy 3:16), he was referring specifically to the Old Testament. When Peter wrote, "Holy men of God spoke as they were moved by the Holy Spirit" (2 Peter 1:21), he was clearly thinking of the Old Testament. When James taught us to be "doers of the word, and not hearers only" (James 1:22), it was the Old Testament he was calling us to obey.

Let me state this clearly. The Old Testament is not a prelude to the Scripture; it is Scripture! In fact, the New Testament can't be fully understood without the Old Testament. The apostle Paul told the Corinthians that the Old Testament stories were given as examples to us. God has provided marvelous illustrations of New Testament truth in these stories.

The Book of Joshua is one of the most dramatic accounts in the entire Bible and is easily one of my favorites. It is the first of a group of books (Joshua—Esther) that form a unified history of Israel, from the time of its entry into Canaan until the time of the Babylonian exile. Scholars note that if the titles were removed from Joshua, Judges, 1 and 2 Samuel, and 1 and 2 Kings, they could be treated as a single book. But of these, Joshua deserves to stand alone. None stir the imagination and move the heart as does this one.

Scholars debate the authorship of this book. Some insist that Joshua wrote part of it. Others say someone else wrote it entirely. No one believes that Joshua wrote it all, because it records his own death as well as events that took place after his death. Regardless of who wrote it, the Book of Joshua appears to be a firsthand account of some of history's greatest moments. These events stand as an encouragement to all who read of them. It is the story of the Hebrew people . . .

- Moving out of the desert wilderness where they had wandered for 40 years

- Moving over the Jordan River that had kept them from a better existence

- Moving into the land that God had promised them hundreds of years before

- Moving on to the life God had for them.

They became an example to us of a people who would not settle for less than the best God had for them.

Before you begin this journey through the Book of Joshua with me, it is important that you know my intent. For anyone looking for a critical exegesis of Joshua, this will not suffice. My intent is by no means academic. I have not attempted to write an erudite work of commentary. Nor did I begin with a desire to research the life that God has promised. This book is the product of my teaching ministry, which is the natural by-product of my devotional life. In simple terms, I began studying the Book of Joshua for me.

As I studied, the Spirit began to flood me with insights into the mind of Joshua and the mind-set of the children of Israel. I began sharing these thoughts with my congregation. The more I studied and taught, the more connection I felt with Joshua, and the more I felt a need to "get on with it." I am tired of wilderness living. I am ready to move out, move over, move in and move on! I doubt that I am alone in this desire. There may be many who are ready to cross, and for those who are, my invitation is simple: "Whosoever will, may come." Canaan awaits.

PART ONE

PREPARING FOR THE PROMISE

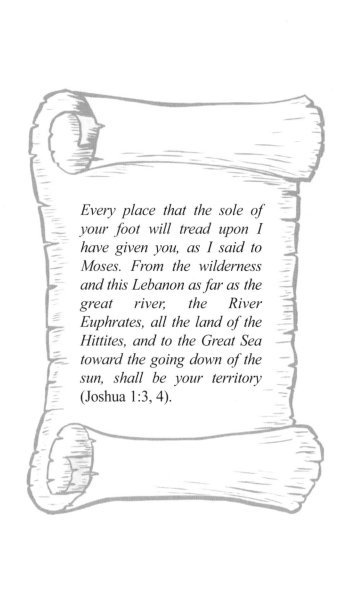

Every place that the sole of your foot will tread upon I have given you, as I said to Moses. From the wilderness and this Lebanon as far as the great river, the River Euphrates, all the land of the Hittites, and to the Great Sea toward the going down of the sun, shall be your territory (Joshua 1:3, 4).

1
What More Is There?

A nyone who knows me well (there are only two, my wife and my mother) will say that I am an inherently restless person. Something inside me seems to say, "There must be more than this." Evidently I am not alone. I have heard this sentiment voiced in a variety of ways by many different people. Surely there must be more—more to love, more to life, more to the faith—just more. Didn't Jesus say something about an abundant life? Doesn't the Bible talk about a joy unspeakable? And what about that peace-that-passes-understanding stuff? What *is* an abundant life? What would joy unspeakable be like? Is peace possible?

When asked these questions, most people will only shrug their shoulders. As one man said, "Life is what it is. I am up in the morning at a time I don't want to be; I fight the traffic to get to a job I don't particularly enjoy; I work all day with people I don't even like, for less pay than I deserve. I go home, eat supper, watch television, go to bed and get up the next morning to start all over again."

19

All of this sounds pessimistic. We could use a dose of good news. So here it is: There is more—much more. The Bible clearly teaches that there is a "promised life." The question is "What more is there?"

Defining the promised life is not easy. Unfortunately, all of us carry baggage in our heads that shades our understanding. Our tendency is to think of the promised life in terms shaped more by our culture than by the Bible. Our images of the abundant life may look more like the commercials on television than the stories in Scripture.

Perhaps the place to start is understanding what the promised life is *not*. I risk losing some readers at this point. When fantasies are challenged and daydreams disrupted, feathers are ruffled. However, ruffled feathers or not, we need to know what we are striving for, so here goes.

What the Promised Life Is *Not*

1. *The promised life is not a life without conflict or problems.* Are you looking for a stress-free existence, a life without hassle? Sorry, no such life is promised. One reason the Book of Joshua makes a good analogy of the promised life, but not a good analogy of heaven, is because it is an account of struggle.

Christians are often surprised to find that spiritual struggles not only continue, but often increase. The promised life has never been, nor will it ever be, a life of ease. Without struggles, there would be no conquest. The promised life will have its share of headaches, but it is a life worth pursuing.

2. *The promised life is not a life of heroic service and extraordinary power.* There are those who think that the life of a Christian should be one in which we

20

experience a miracle a day. As promised-life people, we will not walk on water at will or turn water into wine (iced tea for those of us who live in the Bible Belt). We probably will not win 10 people to Christ every day. No doubt, there *will* be times when God will use us heroically and times when we will witness extraordinary things that can only be explained by the power of God; however, striving to live this kind of life 24/7 will leave us frustrated. The promised life is a life we can live out in everyday events and in the course of ordinary circumstances.

3. *The promised life is not always a life of material wealth.* This is the big one. There probably has not been much disagreement with what I have said thus far, but I can feel the heat rising now. Probably someone reading this is a fan of the latest television preacher to rise to national prominence by telling people that if they come to Jesus, they will have untold riches: money, cars, houses, expensive watches and vacations to exotic lands. Their religious infomercials convince many that the *Master's touch* is the *Midas touch*. No doubt, some have become rich through these ministries, but usually not the ones who are listening to the message. I am not suggesting that God will not prosper His people, I am saying that the pursuit of wealth is not the same as the pursuit of the promised life. In fact, there are those who pursue wealth, get it and then ask, "Is that all there is?"

In recent years, Biblical teachings concerning material prosperity have at best been unbalanced, and at worst completely distorted. Countless thousands have been disillusioned, and some have even dropped out of the faith because of negative effects brought about by a theology that makes financial gain the goal of faith. How different was the mind of Jesus, who said, "It is more blessed to give than to receive" (Acts 20:35).

In *Charisma* magazine (May 2003), James Robison states, "Jesus came that we might have life more abundantly. Those with less than pure motives, or perhaps a lack of clear understanding, mistakenly believe that Jesus came to give us abundance *in* life instead of abundance *of* life. If we understand the true nature of God, we know that He wants to bless and reward His children. God is not opposed to our having things, but He is deeply concerned that things not have us."

What the Promised Life *Is*

So just what is the promised life? We have eliminated some of the popular myths, but is there anything worth pursuing to take their place? Indeed there is.

1. *The promised life is a life that fits*. It is custom-designed for each person. Promised-life people are not pressed out of the same mold. When we pursue the life of promise, we are becoming the one-of-a-kind people God intended us to be. Sadly, cultural conformity sets in . . . even among believers. We talk about individualism, but we pursue lives of bland uniformity. We fear being viewed as peculiar if we don't seek the standard lifestyle that includes two cars, three televisions, two kids, a dog, and a house in the suburbs. Is it just me, or does anyone else think that people of faith look too much alike? If variety is the spice of life, it is no wonder so many believers are bored.

The truth is, God created each of us as originals, not as copies. We often scoff at phrases such as "find yourself" or "discover who you really are," but there is wisdom in these worn-out cliches. Too many people live their lives and never discover themselves. The Bible tells of the uniqueness of God's plan for each of us. In Jeremiah we read, "I know the thoughts that I think toward you, says the Lord, thoughts of peace and not of evil, to give you a future and a hope" (29:11).

The Scriptures promise us that God will give us the desires of our hearts, implying that we can follow our dreams. Many people live lives that do not fit them very well. They are unhappy, unfulfilled and unenthusiastic about life. They are the proverbial square pegs in round holes. Jesus said, "Take My yoke upon you . . . for My yoke is easy and My burden is light" (Matthew 11:29, 30).

These words describe a life that fits. The yoke that is *easy* refers to a yoke that does not chafe or bind the ox. A good paraphrase would be, "Take My yoke upon you, for it will fit you well." For 400 years, the children of Israel lived in a land and culture that did not fit them well. They were strangers in the land of Egypt. There was a Promised Land, however, that would fit them. There was a place for every tribe that fit that tribe's unique needs and character. There was "a place for every tribe, and a tribe for every place." In a similar way, God has a life for everyone and has designed everyone for a life. Do not settle for "good enough" if the life you are living does not fit.

Pursuing the promised life involves asking these questions: What are my gifts? Where do I fit in the body of Christ? The apostle Paul states, "Now you are the body of Christ, and members individually" (1 Corinthians 12:27). Note the word *individually*. In other words, we each have a unique contribution to make. Living a life that does not fit, no matter how good it might look to others, will leave us feeling miserable.

At times, I have found myself living such a life. I am a pastor. Most people think ministers are different from regular folk. Surely pastors are not caught up in climbing the corporate ladder. Wrong. Like everyone else, pastors are prone to measure success by numbers—the bigger the church, the more successful the pastor. Though I tried not to fall into this trap, I found myself fully entangled in this web.

I was the pastor of a 7,000-member church. The ministry was going well. The church was growing, the budgets were being met, and the people seemed satisfied. However, something was not right. As a pastor, I have always been a teacher. My gifts lend themselves to pulpits and podiums. I am not a corporate executive. However, I found myself in the role of CEO, overseeing a $6-million-a-year ministry and managing a staff of 50 people. I did the job reasonably well and was the envy of many of my peers who thought I "had arrived." However, I was not happy. Though I could function in this role, I missed the more personal ministry of teaching and counseling. The church was, and is, a wonderful church—one of the greatest in America—but we simply were not a good match. They did not fit me, and I did not fit them. So when family needs began to mount and the opportunity was presented, I did what many thought foolish: I resigned and stepped out in faith to begin a new ministry.

It was not that I could not handle a large congregation. I had spent the previous eight years successfully leading a 4,000-member congregation, which had nearly doubled during my tenure. Nor was it that the 7,000-member church did not appreciate my teaching ministry.

However, the previous church had different expectations of their pastor. There, I was free to be me. I will always be grateful for my experience, because strangely enough, I believe that God intended me to be there for those two years. But it was not because I fit that lifestyle and ministry; rather, I believe God placed me there to teach me, as well as that congregation, about who we really are. As I pursue the promised life, I am pursuing a life that fits.

The ultimate role model for us is Jesus. He never let anyone determine for Him who He would be. Some wanted Him to be a political ruler; others wanted a military conqueror. However, Jesus knew He had come to be the suffering Savior. He never let other people's expectations govern who He was. He lived the life intended for Him from the foundation of the world.

2. *The promised life is a life that evolves.* It grows and develops over time. When the children of Israel finally conquered the land, their story did not end. It was not even the beginning of the end. It was only the end of the beginning. The story continues for thousands of years. Things changed. Their culture evolved. New forms of government were initiated. New styles of worship emerged. An entire civilization began to grow. The story continues to this very day. That is how God intends a life of promise to be—dynamic, not stagnant. The promised life is not arrived at in a moment of time. It is a process that does not end this side of eternity.

Perhaps the word *evolve* is bothersome. If so, it can be replaced with the words *grow* or *mature*, or if we are brave, we can insert the word *change*. The promised life will never stay the same. We do not strive to arrive; we seek to stay on the journey.

The world is full of people who are not evolving, growing, maturing or changing. They are what they

25

have always been. Frankly, I don't relate well to them. Occasionally, I encounter people I have not seen for years. Sadly, some of them have not changed at all. Recently, I saw an old friend I had not seen in 30 years. We had been teammates on our high school football team. When he saw me, he said, "You haven't changed a bit!" Either he was blind or he was lying. I am sure he meant it as a compliment, but I hope it is not true. Surely after more than 30 years, I have managed to evolve and grow beyond what I was.

We have a plaque that hangs in our home (in the bathroom of all places), that reads as follows:

> What I am is God's gift to me;
> What I become is my gift to God!

A life that does not evolve does not become anything worth giving to God.

3. *The promised life is a life that matters.* It is life that counts for something more than just mere existence. The children of Israel were chosen of God, but they were chosen for a purpose. They were to become a light to the nations that all might know the glory of their God. They were not merely to exist. They were to matter. All life is valuable, but not all people live lives of value.

A grave marker in a cemetery expressed this well. The marker recorded no name, no dates and no identifying information. It simply read: "HE ONCE WAS. HE NOW AIN'T." This epitaph could apply to many people, though most would be surprised to know it. There are many people who are living lives they think matter that will one day be declared "wood, hay, [and] stubble" (1 Corinthians 3:12, KJV).

A life that matters is not necessarily well known. It

may not look particularly successful. However, it will be a life that touches eternity and will continue to count long after it ends.

I recently attended the funeral of a long-time friend who died in an accident. He was only 70 years old and was from all appearances in good health. Pete was a simple man. He was not highly educated. As far as I know, he never held public office. He wrote no books. He never had a television or radio show and, outside the rural community where he lived, few people knew his name. His funeral was one of the best attended I can remember. The church was filled beyond capacity. People were forced to stand outside and listen through an open door. It was obvious that Pete had made a difference in the lives of hundreds of people.

How did he do it? What did he do that mattered to so many people? He smiled a lot. He treated people with dignity. He made people feel important. He taught children in Sunday school and Vacation Bible School. He volunteered to read stories to elementary school students. He loved people and helped them when he could. He served as a role model of gentle, quiet faith. In so doing, he impacted several generations of young people, who are now affecting new generations of young people throughout the community. His name will not go down in the history books, but that does not matter; it is written in the Lamb's Book of Life, and I wouldn't be surprised to find that beside his name are written these words: "A life that mattered."

That is what the promised life is supposed to be.

Discussion Questions

1. How has the culture shaped your image of the promised life?

2. Does the life you are living fit well with your gifts and personality?

3. In what way does your life "matter"?

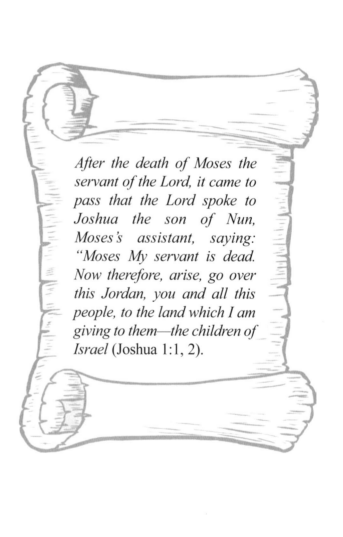

After the death of Moses the servant of the Lord, it came to pass that the Lord spoke to Joshua the son of Nun, Moses's assistant, saying: "Moses My servant is dead. Now therefore, arise, go over this Jordan, you and all this people, to the land which I am giving to them—the children of Israel (Joshua 1:1, 2).

2

The Hardest Part

Joshua 1:1, 2

I am not a very neat person. It is not that I am a complete slob, but I certainly wouldn't be called the tidy type. A plaque on my desk reads, "A cluttered desk is a sign of genius." If this is true, I am another Einstein! Don't get the wrong idea; my study is not a pigsty. There is a path cleared through it. (Of course, there is that one closet I haven't been able to get into for months.) My excuse? I am a busy man. I do not have the time or energy to keep things in order.

That sounds good, but the simple truth is I just do not put a high premium on neatness. Fortunately, I am antisocial enough that I rarely invite people over, so few know of my plight. Occasionally, however, the cleaning bug bites, and I tackle the chaos. This is never easy to do; the problem is knowing where to start.

It seems the hardest part of anything is getting started. (Except for diets. I have started dozens of them.) I spend a great deal of my time counseling people who truly want to change their lives. The most common response I hear is "I just don't know where to start."

WHEN GOOD ENOUGH IS NOT ENOUGH

Living the promised life is no different. Where do we begin? The old proverb is true: "The journey of a thousand miles begins with a single step." The question is, What is that step? The answer will surprise many people. The first step is letting go of the past.

For 400 years, the children of Israel had been in Egypt. Then God sent a man named Moses. Under his leadership, they came out of Egypt, crossed the Red Sea into the wilderness, and eventually came to a place called *Kadesh Barnea*. There they had a decision to make: Will we step over the edge and claim what God has promised us or not? Sadly, they decided they would not.

For the next 40 years, they wandered in the wilderness. In Joshua 1, four decades have passed, Moses has died, and the older generation has passed from the scene. The younger generation has become the older generation and is facing the same choice: Are we going to claim what God has promised us or not? The land lay before them. But moving forward would be difficult until they let go of the past. We are no different.

We Can Only Experience God in the Present Tense

Few things hinder the pursuit of the promised life more than the inability or the unwillingness to live in the present. All of us are, to one degree or another, a product of our past. Unfortunately, many people are also prisoners to their past, and living in the present tense is a struggle. This may have been the case for Joshua as well.

The story begins with an encounter between Joshua and the Lord shortly after the death of Moses. The official time of mourning for the dead was seven days.

However, the death of Moses was observed by the entire nation with 30 days of mourning. The Lord probably spoke to Joshua during or immediately after this time of mourning. I picture Joshua as alone in his thoughts, thinking of the loss of his friend and mentor, when somehow he was made aware of the presence of the Lord. We do not know the exact context of this event. What we do know is that he clearly heard a message that would change his life forever:

> After the death of Moses the servant of the Lord, it came to pass that the Lord spoke to Joshua the son of Nun, Moses's assistant, saying: "Moses My servant is dead" (1:1, 2).

This first statement to Joshua seems harsh, even cold. Why would the Lord say this? Joshua knew that Moses was dead. This was a wake-up call. The Lord was saying to Joshua that a new day—a new era—had begun. We could easily paraphrase this passage to read, "Joshua, forget about the past. Moses is dead. I want to do something new, and I want to do it through you."

God is the God of the living, and life must go on. The idea that God is always the God of the present resonates throughout the Bible. The prophet Isaiah wrote, "Do not remember the former things, nor consider the things of old. Behold, I will do a new thing" (43:18, 19).

We cannot live yesterday, only today. The apostle Paul, writing to the Philippians, said the following:

> Brethren, I do not count myself to have apprehended; but one thing I do, forgetting those things which are behind and reaching forward to those things which are ahead, I press toward the goal for the prize of the upward call of God in Christ Jesus (3:13, 14).

As strange as it might sound, Paul was touting the virtue of forgetfulness. To most of us, forgetfulness is anything but a virtue. And I must confess, my forgetfulness has caused me much grief over the years. I once performed a wedding and forgot the name of the bride. (I learned a valuable lesson that day: Mothers of the bride can be vicious creatures.) Forgetting things can hurt, but not forgetting some things could hurt more.

"Moses My servant is dead." When Moses died, an era ended, and a new day dawned. It was time to move on. Joshua had to let go of Moses and all that the Moses era represented, both positive and negative.

Letting Go of the Positive

Moses' day was a day of great success. He had been the greatest leader the people had ever known. No doubt there were those who thought no one could replace him. It is not hard to imagine what they were thinking: *Moses is dead . . . what are we going to do without him?*

It is important to remember that no individual is indispensable. God's work is bigger than any one person. We pastors can be an arrogant lot. (Please do not shout "amen.") In the back of our minds is the nagging suspicion that we are irreplaceable. But nothing could be further from the truth. Every time God has called me from one place to another, I have worried about how the church would survive without me. However, I have never left a church that subsequently had to shut its doors. In fact, they often go on better without me than with me.

John Wesley was asked what would happen to the Methodist Movement after he died. He replied with a slight indignation, "Sir, I will tell you what will happen: God will bury His workman and get on with His work. Hallelujah, Amen." That is a good statement.

At the time of this writing, Billy Graham continues his ministry. His health is frail and limits what he can do, but Dr. Graham has been the spokesman for Evangelical Christianity for more than 50 years. What will happen when he is no longer with us? The answer is clear and simple: "God will bury His workman and get on with His work. Hallelujah, Amen." No man is indispensable.

The memory of Moses's exploits would be hard to overcome, but Joshua had to let go of the past. It is the same for us. Many people are held back by the success, or perceived success, of the past. John Maxwell says, "The greatest enemy of tomorrow's success is today's success." We tend to rest on our laurels, longing for the good old days.

Churches also do this. Many try to recapture a bygone era, a golden age of the church. The average church in the Bible Belt, where I live, operates ostensibly the way it operated in the post-Depression era. As one pastor said recently, "I am trying to bring my church into the 21st century, and I only have half a century to go." In the Revelation, Jesus declared the church at Sardis to be a dead church, though they had "a reputation of being alive" (3:1, *NIV*).

We do the same individually. When asked to give a testimony of faith, many, if not most, will speak in the past tense. "Tell me about your relationship with Christ," I will ask, only to hear responses such as . . .

- "Well back in '73, I gave my life to the Lord."

- "In '84, I became director of the Adult Department."

- "In '98, I attended the Promise Keepers rally."

I can hear the argument. Someone will say, "What is wrong with lingering in the past? I want to experience God the way I once did." Sorry, you can never experience what God did. You can only experience what God is doing. If you do not experience what God is doing, you will not experience God at all. You only have one option: Get in on what God is doing now, or miss God altogether. Enjoy the memories of what God has done in your life, but do not live by them.

Don Shula did something no other man in modern history has done. The former coach of the Miami Dolphins is the only coach to lead an NFL team to a perfect season and a Super Bowl victory. How did he do it? Shula held to a 24-hour rule. After a game, he allowed himself, his coaches and his players 24 hours to celebrate. But once the 24 hours were over, they had to put it behind them. That is not just good coaching—that is good theology. This is a new day! What does God want to do now? If you want to live the life of promise, you must let go of the past, no matter how good it was.

Letting Go of the Negative

Moses' day was also a day of great failure. We need to remember that Moses did not do all things well. He had some colossal failures as a leader, as well as a man. He was unable to inspire the people to move into Canaan—the one thing he wanted most to do. Under his watch, the people rebelled against the Lord by making a golden calf. He was never able to silence the constant murmuring of the people.

And because of his own lack of submission, he was denied the privilege of entering the land with his people. All of this must have been daunting to Joshua. He knew Moses was a great man. If Moses struggled to succeed, what chance did Joshua have? But a new day had dawned. Moses was dead! There are negatives in each of our lives that will keep us from the life God has for us if we don't let them go.

We must let go of the sins from which we have repented. The word *repented* is the key word. Confessed sins should be forgotten. After all, when our Lord forgives our iniquities, He will not remember our sins (see Jeremiah 31:34). So why should we?

Most spiritually dysfunctional people are living under the condemnation of sins from which they have repented. Many believe that God is still chastening them for their transgression. Let me be clear about this: God does not continue to chasten us for sins for which we have truly repented. The Scriptures describe God as our *Abba*, an Aramaic word that means "affectionate father." What kind of father would continue to chasten his children long after they have repented and been restored? The apostle John said it so well: "If we confess our sins, He is faithful and just to forgive us our sins and to cleanse us from all unrighteousness" (1 John 1:9). Guilt for sins already forgiven is not from the Father. It is a spiritual attack.

We must let go of the mistakes we have made. We all struggle with sin and make mistakes. I regard sins as willful transgressions. Mistakes are, more often than not, lapses in judgment. Is it just me, or does anyone else suffer from momentary lapses into stupidity? I can do the dumbest things. I find myself asking, "What was I thinking?"

The mistakes of the past can keep us from pursuing

37

the life God has promised. These can be painful and embarrassing experiences. In an attempt to avoid them in the future, we retreat into our shell and play it safe. That is an even bigger mistake. Learn from your mistakes, but don't live by them. Let go of the past.

It is not only important that we put the sins and mistakes of our past behind us, it is just as essential that we allow others to do the same. If we are going to claim the grace of God for ourselves, we must be willing to extend it to others who have also struggled and failed.

At the conclusion of a speaking engagement, a young woman named Sandy asked to speak to me. I had been talking about the forgiveness of God that cleanses us and makes us whole. In the course of my remarks, I referred to the church as the reservoir of God's mercy, a place where those wounded by sin can come and bathe in healing and restoring grace. She was visibly disturbed by my remarks. Her experience with the church was nothing like my description. Sandy had suffered greatly in life and had made her share of mistakes. She had grown up attending a small church and was well-grounded in the faith. However, an abusive and alcoholic father caused her to question her beliefs. By the age of 17, she had left home, and at 19, she met and fell in love with an older married man. He had convinced her that he loved her and wanted to marry her as soon as his divorce was final. She agreed to move in with him until they could be married.

The wedding day came, followed by three successive pregnancies. But Sandy's happy life quickly turned sour. She found herself trapped in another abusive relationship with an alcoholic man. Soon after the birth of their first child, he began beating her. Not knowing what to do, she stayed with him, but her situation only grew worse. The abuse continued and grew more violent after the birth of each successive child. Eventually, he began to turn his rage on the children. Finally, unable to tolerate the abuse any longer, Sandy filed for divorce.

Taking her children with her, she returned to her hometown. With no place else to turn, she went back to her church. *Surely there I will find a safe haven and people who care*, she thought. But the church of her childhood was not as she remembered. As she entered the sanctuary, no one spoke to her. When she inquired about a Sunday school class, she was informed that there was none for single mothers and that she probably would not feel comfortable in the only couple's class they had for people her age. Sandy decided that if there was no class for her, she would volunteer to work with the babies in the nursery. But when she asked if she could do so, she was informed that the church didn't allow divorced people to serve.

To this day, I can see the painful expression on her face. *Is this really how Christ would have treated her?* When Christ encountered people in their sin, His first response was to offer grace. Shouldn't that be our first response as well? Let go of the negative things of the past, and let others do so as well. We must not let yesterday cripple us today and rob us of tomorrow.

Letting Go Is Hard to Do

That leaves us with one question: How do we let go of the past? I do not wish to imply that it will be easy. Some people spend a lifetime trying to overcome their past. It may require extensive counseling for some. Others may need to make painful restitution. But for most of us, the solution is relatively simple. (Notice I said simple, not easy.) We let go of the past by moving forward with our lives. This was the message to Joshua.

> After the death of Moses the servant of the Lord, it came to pass that the Lord spoke to Joshua the son of Nun, Moses' assistant, saying, "Moses My servant is dead. Now therefore, arise, go over this Jordan, you and all this people" (Joshua 1:1, 2).

The most important words in this passage are the words *now, therefore, arise* and *go*. How do we let go of the past? We live our lives in the present and toward the future. The apostle Paul expressed this same sentiment in his Philippians challenge—"forgetting those things which are behind . . . I press toward the goal" (3:13, 14). As simplistic as it sounds, Paul is saying the way to get over the past is by getting on with life. We often hear the statement "Everyone has a past." This is not true. In fact, the truth is that no one has a past or, for that matter, a future. The past does not exist—it is only a memory. The future has not yet happened—it is only a hope. All we have is the present.

Let me speak pointedly. Has life been good? Wonderful! The question now is, What next? With God, the best is yet to be. Has life been hard? I am so sorry. Now pick up the pieces, and get on with it. It really is a choice. What are you waiting for, life number two? That is called eternity. The two most important truths I know are these: Jesus is Lord, and life is short!

"Moses My servant is dead. Now therefore, arise!"

Discussion Questions

1. To what degree are you the product of or a prisoner to your past?

2. To what degree is your church a product of or a prisoner to its past?

3. Is it possible to completely let go of the past?

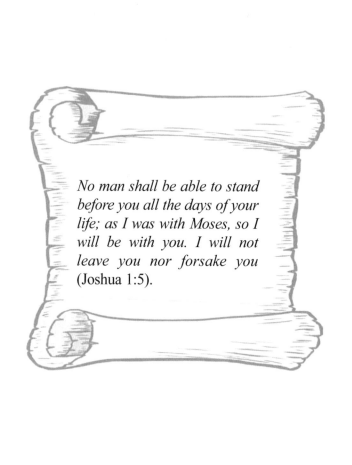

No man shall be able to stand before you all the days of your life; as I was with Moses, so I will be with you. I will not leave you nor forsake you (Joshua 1:5).

3

Never Alone

My personal library has hundreds of volumes on subjects ranging from existential philosophy to elemental zoology. As an avid reader, I pride myself on having books that are so complex the authors who wrote them don't even know what they are about. But of all the books in my collection, one is my favorite and has taught me much about God. It is not an erudite work of theology. It is not one of the classics of Christian literature. Rather, it is a tiny book titled *Children's Letters to God.* I am amazed at the insight children have that we "mature" folk seem to have lost. Here are some of my favorites from the book:

- "Dear God, How do you know you are God?"

- "Dear God, who takes your place when you are on vacation?"

- "Dear God, are you and the pastor friends? He seems to think so."

Of all the letters or statements in this wonderful little

43

volume, none has touched me as much as the letter written by a little girl named Nora:

- "Dear God, I'm not lonely anymore now that I've learned about You."

Wow! What a statement. That little girl had discovered one of the greatest truths of the faith: We are never alone, never alone, no never, ever alone! This is good news.

Loneliness is a major issue in our lives. Thomas Wolfe said, "Loneliness is not a peculiarity of our time, rather the central fact of existence." Paul Tournier seemed to disagree. He called loneliness "the most devastating malady of the age." Billy Graham was once asked, "What are the biggest problems facing people today?" To the surprise of his questioner, he replied, "Everywhere I go, I encounter people who are lonely."

Many of you suffer from loneliness, and no one knows how alone you feel. You are surrounded by people, yet you feel as though you have no one to connect with deeply. H.G. Wells, at his 65th birthday celebration, lifted a wineglass and said, "I am 65 and all alone."

Loneliness is especially prevalent in leadership roles. The old saying "It is lonely at the top" is true. Joshua must have felt the loneliness of leadership. As the new leader of nearly 2 million people, he had just been commissioned to do what even Moses, his mentor, could not do. What a lonely position. Joshua needed something to hold on to. He needed something big! He got it in the form of a promise from God: "As I was with Moses, so I will be with you. I will not leave you nor forsake you" (Joshua 1:5).

I love the promises of Scripture. Paul wrote, "For all

the promises of God in Him are Yes, and in Him Amen, to the glory of God through us" (2 Corinthians 1:20). Paraphrase: If God says He will do something, He will do it. F.B. Meyer said, "If any promise of God should fail, the heavens would clothe themselves with sackcloth . . . a hollow wind would moan through a ruined creation the awful fact that God can lie." But God cannot lie . . . does not lie . . . will not lie.

Of all the promises, none is sweeter to the believer than the promise that God is with us. This same promise was echoed by the writer of Hebrews:

> For He Himself has said, "I will never leave you nor forsake you." So we may boldly say: "The Lord is my helper; I will not fear. What can man do to me?" (13:5, 6).

Without the knowledge that God is with us, life will traumatize us. What did this promise mean to Joshua? Perhaps it will help to take it apart and examine what Joshua heard.

A God Who Plays No Favorites

"As I was with Moses, so I will be with you" (Joshua 1:5). Our God is an equal-opportunity God. He would be in Joshua's life just as He had been in the life of Moses. Joshua must have been suffering from a case of "Who, me?" No doubt he was thinking, *Moses was a great leader, but I am no Moses.* Joshua had admired Moses and perhaps even wanted to be like him. But Moses was special, wasn't he? He was different, wasn't he? No, he was not. Moses was just a man upon whom rested the hand of God. He was not chosen because he was special. He was special because he was chosen. I love the words to that old gospel

45

song, "It is no secret what God can do. What He's done for others, He'll do for you." I need to know that.

Sometimes I suffer from "Who, me?" I know that others can be used of God, but I am not sure that He can do much with me. I am no Billy Graham; I am no Mother Teresa. But none of that matters. God plays no favorites. This does not mean that He will anoint everyone the same . . . or give the same ministry or visibility to all. But He does promise to give each of us authority in our own realm of influence. These first words must have given Joshua great courage.

One side note: God plays no favorites, but He does have intimates. Clearly, there are some who are more intimately acquainted with God than others. The key to knowing God intimately is to hide His Word in your heart.

> This Book of the Law shall not depart from your mouth, but you shall meditate in it day and night, that you may observe to do according to all that is written in it. For then you will make your way prosperous, and then you will have good success. Have I not commanded you? Be strong and of good courage; do not be afraid, nor be dismayed, for the Lord your God is with you wherever you go (vv. 8, 9).

A God Who Will Not Fail

The second word Joshua heard *from God* was that He would not leave him. At this point, I prefer the older translation that says, "I will not fail thee" (v. 5, KJV). The Hebrew word *raphah* (pronounced *raw-faw*), carries with it the idea of disappointment, letting someone down. What Joshua heard was that the Lord would never

46

disappoint him, never let *him* down, never fail *him*. This
was an incredibly important message for Joshua to hear.
He was facing a monumental task. He knew he could not
fulfill his role unless God led him. But *with* God, he
could do all he was being led to do.

I need to know this as well. So many times, I have
failed on my own. Frankly, I don't have much confidence in my own abilities. I did once, but then life happened. As I assess my life, I realize that I don't do much
for God. But what has always amazed me is how much
God does through me.

My greatest fear is that I might fail Him. But my faith
rises when I accept the liberating truth that God will not
fail me. Only then can I venture in faith beyond my abilities knowing that "with men this is impossible, but with
God all things are possible" (Matthew 19:26). This word
had to rejuvenate Joshua's courage and give him great
confidence.

A God Who Will Not Forsake

There was a third word that Joshua heard. The promise said, "I will not leave you nor forsake you" (v. 5). If
the first word gave him *courage*, and the second word
gave him *confidence*, this third word gave him *comfort*.
To forsake means "to abandon or desert." This was God's
promise that He would never leave Joshua out on a limb.
He would always be there—in good times and bad—
when Joshua did well or when he blew it. What a comfort!

In Hebrews 13, the Greek language adds to the impact
of the promise. The promise in Joshua simply says "I
will *not* forsake you," but the writer of Hebrews states

more emphatically, "I will never leave you nor forsake you" (v. 5). Scholars tell us that the word *never* is actually a combination of five negatives. The more literal translation would be "I will never, no not ever, no never ever ever leave you or forsake you."

The task ahead was not only monumentally difficult—it was also extremely dangerous. On occasion, it would be heartbreaking as well. The promised life can be that way. But Joshua would never, no not ever, no never ever ever be alone in his journey . . . and neither will you.

A young woman shared her sad testimony with me. Married to the love of her life, she could not have been happier. She sensed nothing wrong in the marriage until one morning she awoke to find her husband gone and a note saying that he was filing for divorce. She did not see him again until she saw him in court. The judge granted the divorce. When she walked out of the courthouse, she stood at the bottom of the steps and watched the man she loved get into a car with a woman she had never seen before. She said, "At that moment, I felt more alone than I have felt in my life. I think I felt something of what Christ must have felt on the cross, abandoned by all." People may forsake us in life, but our Lord never will. What does this mean to you?

You are never alone in your stress. There are times when the stress of life seems more than you can handle, and no one seems to understand. I deal with many men who feel as though the weight of the world is on their shoulders. A common response is "I feel trapped. There is no way out. My family depends on me. My wife does not understand what it is like to be the one responsible for providing for the family." The feeling of being trapped in stressful situations is common in today's society. It may be the number one reason why men are leaving their families. Many men say, "I have had all I can take." The underlying problem many of these men are dealing with is a sense of loneliness. They can't talk to their wives about their feelings without creating anxiety in them.

Women feel no less stress in their lives. They complain that their husbands do not understand them. The truth is . . . they don't. Women handle this stress better than men by seeking friendships to overcome their loneliness. In either case, the good news is, You are *never* alone. There is a God who loves you and understands what no mate ever could. On many occasions, the only thing that keeps me going is the promise that *I am not alone*. The Scripture says I have "a friend who sticks closer than a brother" (Proverbs 18:24).

You are never alone in your fear. Life can be scary. None of my childhood fears compare with the feelings I experience sometimes as an adult. One of the loneliest experiences is awaiting surgery. Your family has kissed you good-bye and has promised to be there when you wake up. The nurses who wheel you to the operating room try to relieve your anxiety with small talk. They tell you that they are right there with you. All around you technicians are getting everything ready. You have never been less alone—yet never lonelier. It is just you and the Lord. But He is there.

You are never alone in your sin. The Bible states that your sin separates you from God, but rest assured your sin does not separate God from you. In moments of moral failure, God is with you. God does not abandon His children when they sin any more than I would abandon my children when they disobey me. Their behavior may separate them from me, but it will never separate me from them.

49

You are never alone in your failure. For me the loneliest experience in my life was the moment of my greatest failure. Alone in a decision that I knew could damage, or even end, a successful career, I felt as though I was living on a deserted island with nothing to do but rehearse my shame. It was only the sense of God's presence that enabled me to get up every morning and face life.

You are never alone in your suffering. When the chemotherapy has cost you all your hair, when the nausea is so intense you think dying would be better than living, you have a Father in heaven who understands how you feel. Call on Him, and He will hear.

You are never alone in your sorrow. When your heart is breaking over the loss of the most important person in your life, you are not alone. When I minister to someone who has just lost a mate, I cannot honestly say, "I know what you are going through." I have never had to endure such grief, and I pray I never do. It may sound strange, but it is actually a blessing to men that God designed most of us to die younger than our wives. It may seem selfish, but I personally pray that God will give my wife and me many years together, but I hope He allows me to die first. I have always thought that she is far more able to live without me than I her. I don't know what I would do without her.

Over the years, I have heard numerous testimonies of the painful loss of a mate. One man, whose wife passed two years before, told me, "Pastor, when I get up in the morning it takes me 30 minutes to realize that she is not here." A 68-year-old widow said, "I thought I was over the death of my husband. After all, it has been over a year since he died. But the other day I was at the kitchen sink washing dishes when I opened the cabinet to put up a plate. There it was: my husband's favorite coffee mug. I don't know how it happened, but the next thing I knew, I was on the floor in a fetal position, crying like a baby." Another woman said she was unable to break the habit of setting a place for her late husband at the dinner table. A widower, who had been married over 40 years before his wife died, said at night he lies diagonally across the bed so that the bed will not seem so empty.

There are other sorrows. One of the most painful of all life's experiences is the death of a child. There is something that seems unnatural about it. If you have endured such sorrow, you were not alone. I am never, no not ever, no never ever ever, alone in my sorrow. And neither are you.

I will never forget the scene. It was late, almost midnight. Earlier that evening, I had received a phone call informing me that the father of a church member had just suffered a massive heart attack. In his late 50s, he was, from all appearances, the picture of health. The family had quickly assembled at the hospital, including his children, his wife, and his elderly mother who was well into her 80s. I ministered for a while and excused myself, telling the family to call me if things changed. A little after 11 p.m., my phone rang again telling me that the doctor had sent word for the family to all assemble in the waiting room. I rushed back to the hospital. By the time I arrived, the doctor had just informed them that although they did all they could, it was not enough, their loved one had died. The room was full of sorrow. The wife was weeping uncontrollably. Her two grown sons were kneeling next to her trying to console her. A daughter was standing in a corner with a stunned look on her face. It was obvious to me they were all in shock.

Suddenly someone broke through the sobbing and asked, "Where is Grandma?" Amid the grief, the little 85-year-old grandmother had disappeared. Everyone began to frantically look around to see where she had gone. Suddenly someone said, "Shhhhh! Be quiet, listen." As we grew silent, we heard something coming from a darkened room attached to the waiting area. I stepped at the door and pushed it open—just enough to peer in. There inside was the little grandmother sitting in a rocking chair staring out the window. As I stepped in, I heard her trembling voice, muffled by occasional sobs, softly singing:

> I come to the garden alone,
>   While the dew is still on the roses,
> And the voice I hear falling on my ear,
>   The Son of God discloses.
> And He walks with me and He talks with me,
>   And He tells me I am His own.
> And the joy we share as we tarry there,
>   None other has ever known.

"I will never, no not ever, no never ever ever forsake you." If there were nothing else, this truth alone makes the promised life worth pursuing.

Discussion Questions

1. Do you agree that, though God may have intimates, He has no favorites?

2. If God is always with us, why are we so often unaware of His presence?

3. What can we do to heighten our awareness of God's presence?

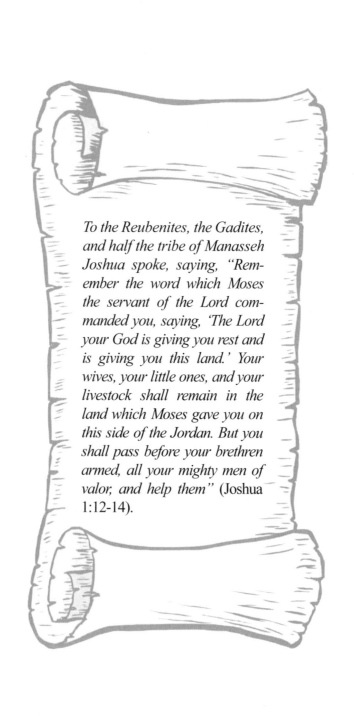

To the Reubenites, the Gadites, and half the tribe of Manasseh Joshua spoke, saying, "Remember the word which Moses the servant of the Lord commanded you, saying, 'The Lord your God is giving you rest and is giving you this land.' Your wives, your little ones, and your livestock shall remain in the land which Moses gave you on this side of the Jordan. But you shall pass before your brethren armed, all your mighty men of valor, and help them" (Joshua 1:12-14).

4

Please Make Yourself Uncomfortable

Joshua 1:10-18

I have an old pair of shoes that are in pitiful condition. There is a hole in the bottom of one, and the sides are running over the edge of both. The left one has a torn seam. The heels are worn down. They look awful, not to mention the smell. They do not offer good support, and I have been told that they may not be good for the alignment of my spine. However, none of that matters. I wear them almost every day. Why? The answer is simple: they are comfortable. I like things to be comfortable. I like comfortable shoes. I like a comfortable chair. I like a comfortable bed. I like comfortable (loose) pants.

Comfort is good, right? Yes, comfort is good. Comfort is always good, right? No, comfort is *not* always good. Comfort in an old pair of shoes is one thing, but when it comes to the promised life, it is something else entirely.

Many of us, I fear, wear life like an old pair of shoes. We don't venture out. We rarely take a chance. We sacrifice nothing. We accomplish little and experience few victories. But none of these things seem to matter, because we are comfortable. We have found our comfort zone and have settled in. Some people even believe the promised life is a life lived in comfort. Nothing could be further from the truth.

The comfort zone is just another name for the "good-enough" syndrome. There are, in fact, two kinds of people: the comfort-zone crowd and the promised-life people.

Comfort-zone people are among the most difficult people to lead. In Joshua 1:12-18, Joshua encountered people who had found their comfort zone. The passage alludes to an encounter that occurred some months before—between Moses and the leaders of three tribes: Reuben, Gad and the half tribe of Manasseh (see Numbers 32).

These three tribes found a spot on the east side of the Jordan River that suited their needs. It was not as fertile as the land on the other side, but to them it seemed good enough. Their leaders informed Moses that they had no intention of going into the Promised Land. Understandably, Moses was upset at this news, but he soon acquiesced. After all, he could not make them claim what was rightfully theirs. But Moses required one thing of them. When the time came for the rest of the people to cross over and conquer the land, they had to help. In fact, they not only had to help, they also had to lead the way. In this passage, Joshua reminds them of their obligation. This is a peculiar story but one that speaks to us today. Claiming what is rightfully ours may require that we become uncomfortable.

An Awesome Privilege

We can go as far with God as we want to go. This is an awesome and mind-boggling privilege. Clearly, the

Promised Land was the children of Israel's inheritance. But if they did not want it, it would not be forced on them. God is a gentleman. He will not force His will on anyone. I know that plays havoc with the theology of some people. Some suggest that He does. As one man said to me, "I never wanted to be a preacher, but God made me become one." Nonsense; his mother may have made him, but God did not. We can go as far with God as we wish—limited only by our own desire.

This privilege has positive implications. It means if I want to go far and deep, I can. In fact, I can go as far and as deep as anyone else. Remember, God plays no favorites. On occasion I have encountered those who appear to have an intense and intimate relationship with the Lord. Their walk seems so close, and their faith so vivid. When I see these people, I long to be like them. The good news is, I can. God never limits my relationship with Him. Quite the contrary, He states repeatedly that He will meet me at the point of my desire:

- "Blessed are those who hunger and thirst for righteousness, for they shall be filled" (Matthew 5:6).

- "Delight yourself also in the Lord, and He shall give you the desires of your heart" (Psalm 37:4).

- "You will seek Me and find Me, when you search for Me with all of your heart" (Jeremiah 29:13).

Here is the truth: God will not limit your relationship with Him. God has a wonderful plan for your life, and you can follow that plan as far as you wish.

This privilege has negative implications as well. If you do not want to go deeper with God, you will not be forced to do so. If you are satisfied with the mediocre and mundane, you can have it. This was the problem with the Reubenites, Gadites and half the tribe of Manasseh. They were happy where they were and with what they had. This is a story repeated often in the faith. So many Christians have gone as far as they want to go. They come to church to get their weekly reminder that God loves them, and then they go about their business. I don't know how much of God you experience, but I can guarantee you that it is as much as you want.

We often complain of the lack of spirit in the church. Where is God when we meet together? Doesn't the Bible promise that where two or three are gathered in His name, there His presence will be (see Matthew 18:20)? The truth is, most of our churches are spiritually dry and happily so. We talk about revival and renewal. We say we want God to pour out His Spirit upon us, but in fact, most churches would not know what to do if He did. We have as much of God as we want in our churches. Any more of Him would disrupt our comfort. It is comfortable to come to church, go through familiar routines and sing familiar songs. We take comfort in knowing that the service will start on time and end on time. We like knowing what to expect, and if God really shows up, it might disrupt our well-planned service.

The sad thing is we tend to congregate in churches of like-minded people. In other words, comfort-zone people go to comfort-zone churches. Jesus warned against this in two letters written to the churches of Asia Minor in Revelation. First, there was the warning to the church of Ephesus:

> "I know your works, your labor, your patience, and that you cannot bear those who are evil. And you have tested

those who say they are apostles and are not, and have found them liars; and you have persevered and have patience and have labored for My name's sake and have not become weary. Nevertheless I have this against you, you have left your first love" (2:2-4).

In many ways, the church at Ephesus was a good church—the kind that would have a big membership today. It was a hardworking church that labored long for the faith—an orthodox church that would not put up with false teaching. However, the problem was that they were a comfort-zone church. They had left their first love. They had settled into a comfortable pattern with no passion. They were sincere, but their fervor was not there. In other words, they were comfortable. But they were not alone. Second, there was the warning to the church at Laodicea.

"These things says the Amen, the Faithful and True Witness, the Beginning of the creation of God: I know your works, that you are neither cold nor hot. I could wish you were cold or hot. So then, because you are lukewarm, and neither cold nor hot, I will vomit you out of My mouth" (3:14-16).

This is an incredible indictment. To paraphrase, this church made Jesus sick. What was the problem? These people had grown comfortable—much too comfortable. This is the condition of most of our churches and many, if not most, who call themselves Christian. Not hot, not cold, just comfortably lukewarm. Let me repeat: We have as much of God as we desire. He has given us the awesome privilege of going as far with Him as we want to go. How do we lose our passion and settle into comfort zones? The answer is not simple. There is a myriad of things that cause us to settle.

1. *Sin shakes our faith.* The guilt of sin has caused many a person to feel unworthy. It causes us to lose faith in our faith. So we settle down into a life that requires none.

2. *Possessions dull our desire.* The apostle John warned, "Do not love the world or the things in the world" (1 John 2:15). But most of us do. Paul spoke of a man named Demas who deserted the cause, "having loved this present world" (2 Timothy 4:10). That sounds familiar. Timothy was told no good soldier of the Cross "entangles himself with the affairs of this life" (2:4). But most of us have done just that. Our taste for the promised life has been dulled by our taste for the present life.

3. *Ignorance causes us to settle.* Many don't know that there is more to the faith than just going to church. For them, being a Christian means living a life in which they do no harm (see Romans 13:10). What more would God have for them? This is becoming more and more the case. I am amazed at the Biblical ignorance of our times. Not just ignorance outside the church—I am speaking of ignorance *inside* the church.

4. *Life robs us of our dream.* The bottom line is, these people have lost their dream. Most people I have known over the years come into the faith with zeal and passion, but somewhere many of them lose the dream. In the Joshua account, the tribes of Reuben, Gad and half the tribe of Manasseh had lost or given up their dream of a better land. The dream seemed too difficult to achieve, so they settled down and zoned out.

In his groundbreaking book, *The Purpose Driven Church*, Rick Warren struck a chord with many when he

dared to ask, "What is the purpose for which our churches exist?" I doubt the average church has asked that question since its founding. Churches without purpose are
comfort-zone churches without a dream. Church growth
experts speak of the "single generation church." This is a
church that forms and for a single generation impacts the
kingdom of God. Then it settles into a comfortable pattern of doing things. The church soon forgets its original
purpose. The dream of the founding members is only a
distant memory recorded in the archives. This church
may exist for another 50 to 100 years, but it does little
that matters in the Kingdom. Many a church has died in
the comfort zone.

A Dangerous Choice

*Living in comfort zones can be hazardous to your spir-
itual health.* Living on the east side of the Jordan could,
and ultimately would, prove to be a dangerous choice for
these tribes. When Moses allowed them to choose, it was
not without warning. This was a serious choice that
would have ramifications not only for them, but also for
their children and their children's children. Comfort-
zone Christians seldom realize the danger of their choice.
In fact, they often believe the comfort zone will keep
them out of danger. There are three great dangers facing
those who choose to live in the comfort zone.

1. *Causing others to fall short.* This will not be a pleasant nor popular thing to suggest, but here goes. As a
believer, you are not in the faith alone. In other words, it
is not only about you. Your unwillingness to go all the
way with God can and will affect others. At best, you
will be a discouragement and, at worst, an obstacle to

those who want all God has for them. Many a child has burned with desire to go deep in their faith, only to find their passion cooled by parents who are comfortable right where they are. The same is true for wives who long for spiritual intimacy but face cold indifference to matters of faith from their husbands, who claim to be the spiritual head of their home. This plays out more often in churches than anywhere else. God is working to revive His church, but many within simply don't want to be bothered. These people do not think of themselves as hindering revival, but in fact, they are the very reason revival is so desperately needed. If you belong to a church, you have an obligation. You may not be interested in going far with God, but you must do your share to help those who are.

2. *The failure to maintain.* Spiritual atrophy sets in. Choosing to go no further with God would be one thing if once we made the choice we were able to maintain that level of faith. The truth is, however, that with God, we cannot stand still. Either we move forward, or we slide back. We either prosper or decline, progress or digress. History records that these tribes were not able to maintain their comfortable existence. They found themselves unable to fortify their position. The result was these tribes were the first to fall. History records the sad account of how these tribes were the first to be captured when the Assyrians invaded Israel. Once captured, they never returned. So often this is the case.

The first to fall to spiritual attack, and often apostasy, are the comfort-zone people. Church rolls are full of such casualties of the spiritual war. Thinking they were playing it safe by not "going off the deep end," they find themselves aground in the shallows, unable to avoid the

Enemy's attack. Empty, alone, discouraged and depressed, they have fallen far from even the mediocre faith they once knew. Many will wonder why God has abandoned them. But the truth is, they simply did not go with Him.

3. *Missing the best God has for us.* The third danger is perhaps the most profound. Simply stated, if we stay in the comfort zone, we will miss the best God has for us. At any moment in my Christian life I can say to the Lord, "I have gone as far as I want to go. I can't stand it, the conflict is too big, the struggle too great." It is my privilege to go as far as I want to go and no further. But God's best is rarely found in the comfort zone.

Napoleon Hill said, "Cherish your visions and your dreams as they are the children of your soul, the blueprints of your ultimate achievements." It is tragic when churches or individuals give up their dream and settle into comfort-zone faith. The saddest people I know are people nearing the end of their life who sit around talking about what might have been. These are comfort-zone people who realize that they have missed God's best, and it is too late to do anything about it.

Let me tell you my philosophy of life. I believe all of life should be lived in preparation for the last five conscience minutes of existence. I want to live my life in such a way that when I come to those last five minutes, I will look back without regret and look forward with hope. I do not want to look back and ask, "What if?" And I don't want to look ahead and fear what's next. I will never accomplish this if I live life in the comfort zone. And neither will you.

What is your dream? Have you given up on it? Have you packed it away like an old sweater you can't bare to part with but doubt you will ever wear again? Maybe it is time to pull it out, shake the dust off and dare to dream again. Are you living your life like you'd wear an old pair of shoes? Don't let comfort keep you from accepting what is rightfully yours.

Discussion Questions

1. To what extent is your comfort zone affecting your faith?

2. If it is true that we rarely meet God in the comfort zone, what are the implications for your life and your church?

3. Paul declared that he had learned to be content in whatever state he was in (see Philippians 4:11). What is the difference between being content and living in a comfort zone?

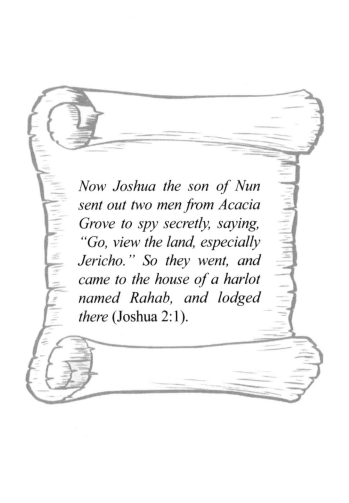

Now Joshua the son of Nun sent out two men from Acacia Grove to spy secretly, saying, "Go, view the land, especially Jericho." So they went, and came to the house of a harlot named Rahab, and lodged there (Joshua 2:1).

5

A Grace Thing

L et me describe a few people to you. As I do, consider what each has in common with the other:

- An arrogant, young agnostic
- A washed-up ex-baseball player
- A farm boy who was thought to have little or, at best, average potential
- A young man who spent most of his time and money on women
- An uneducated shoe clerk
- A teenage girl pregnant out of wedlock

It is not difficult to connect the dots between these people. Each is a person with whom "proper" folk would
have little association—the kind who fall through the
cracks of society. You know the type. When you see them
on the street, you pass by them quickly without making
eye contact. These are the outcasts . . . the fringe crowd .
. . the losers. We could call them "throwaway" people.

67

Throwaway People

Follow their stories however, and you will discover they have something else in common. Each was a throwaway person who was recycled by the grace of God.

- The arrogant, young agnostic was Charles Finney, the great revivalist.

- The washed-up ex-baseball player was Billy Sunday—the first man to preach the gospel to over 1 million people.

- The farm boy who was thought to have little potential was Billy Graham, who needs no introduction.

- The young man who spent most of his time and money on women was Saint Augustine—one of the most influential theologians of all time.

- The uneducated shoe clerk was Dwight L. Moody—a man used by God to shake two continents for Christ.

- The pregnant teenager was Mary, who gave birth to our Lord.

Learn this lesson: Our God delights in taking nobodies and making somebodies of them. He loves to do extraordinary things in the life of ordinary people. Joshua 2 is an account of such a person—one of life's throwaways recycled by grace. This is a parenthetic passage—a passage of Scripture that interrupts the flow of the content like a time-out in the main story. In Joshua 1, the children of Israel are preparing to cross over the Jordan River and in chapter 3, they cross over. But in chapter 2, you have this odd little story about a woman named Rahab, a woman the Scripture calls a *harlot*. This is the story of a woman of the streets—a hooker, a prostitute.

Let me set the story in context. Joshua sent two spies into Jericho. Word of their presence reached the king. A manhunt was undertaken to find them, but the men found refuge in the home of Rahab, who hid them from the authorities. Before they left, she asked them to spare her and all her family when the Israelites invaded. The two men gave their word. They promised that if she would gather all her family into her home and hang a scarlet cord out the window to mark her house, all would be spared. Later when the walls of Jericho fell, Rahab's house, which was on the wall, remained, and none in it were harmed.

This is a story of a prostitute, but there is more to the story; Rahab becomes more than a prostitute. Follow the story beyond the Book of Joshua. Later she marries a prince of Israel; the prostitute becomes a princess. In fact, she becomes more than just a princess. As a result of her marriage, Rahab the harlot becomes the great-great-grandmother of David, the king. Isn't that fantastic? If you follow the story into the New Testament, Matthew 1 includes her as one of the ancestors of Jesus. Can you imagine such a thing? A prostitute, a harlot, a hooker is now in the lineage of our Lord. What a fantastic turn of events! Who would have thought it possible?

Why is this account in Scripture? Why did the writer think this event warranted the time and space to record it? Bible scholars have speculated this over the years. Many elaborate explanations have been given. I think the answer is simple. Rahab is a marvelous picture of what I call the "grace-faith" dynamic. She serves to remind us that the promised life is a gift of God totally undeserved—totally

unmerited—entered into by grace through faith. Do you
ever feel unworthy? Do you sometimes feel that other
people deserve the promised life, but you do not? The
story of Rahab is just for you.

It occurs to me that I have been using a phrase that
may be a little misleading. From time to time, I have
talked about "claiming what is rightfully yours." I fear
some might mistakenly get the idea that they deserve all
that God has promised, or that they can somehow earn
the right to a better life. Let me be clear. The promised
life is rightfully yours only because God, in His infinite
grace, has chosen to give it. You don't deserve it. I don't
deserve it. It is a grace thing, entered into by the dynamic of faith.

I love that old song "Amazing Grace." You simply
cannot mess it up no matter how you do it. You can bang
it out on a honky-tonk piano, or it can be played by a
symphony orchestra. You can use bagpipes or harmoni-
cas. Little children can sing it, or opera stars can perform
it. It is one of those songs that is always appropriate. I
love to sing about grace, and I love to preach about the
grace of God. I have discovered, however, that grace is
an idea that people find hard to grasp. In fact, there are
the two doctrines—grace and faith—and people have a
hard time with both of them. The Bible says we are saved
by grace through faith (Ephesians 2:8). Have you ever
tried to explain that to somebody, only to have them
glaze over and say, "I don't get it"?

A Work of Grace

In many ways, grace is one of those things that can't be
explained fully. Some things in life must be experienced

to understand. Try explaining the color blue to someone who has never seen blue. If you have not experienced blueness, you cannot understand blue. Grace is like that. If you have never experienced it, you simply can't understand it. But once you have experienced it, you know that there is nothing else like it in the world. However, there are certain things about grace you must understand before you can experience it.

1. *Grace seeks you where you are.* Long before Rahab encountered God in her life, He had already begun working in her heart. The grace of God preceded the faith of Rahab. As you read the story, you discover that she does not seek God, but God seeks her. He sends the spies to her. When they encounter Rahab, they discover that she already believes. They don't have to convince, convict or persuade her. Rahab, the prostitute of Jericho, who was a harlot and a pagan, has already come to believe that there is only one true God. This is the preliminary work of grace preparing the way.

We get this backward. Most of us think that faith initiates grace. We think that we put our faith in God, and then God activates His grace toward us. The Bible teaches that God activates His grace toward us so that we can begin to have faith in Him. The Scripture teaches that faith is a gift from God. The apostle Paul said, "There is none who seeks after God" (Romans 3:11). Jesus made this statement, "You did not choose Me, but I chose you" (John 15:16). In chapter 14, Jesus said, "No one comes to the Father except through Me" (v. 6). But earlier in John 6, He said, "No one can come to Me unless it has been granted to him by My Father" (v. 65). Grace initiates faith. In 1 John, we read, "We love Him because He first loved us" (4:19).

I can pinpoint a moment in time when I trusted my life to Christ. But long before that moment in time, the grace of God was already working, stirring faith in me. Understand salvation is instantaneous, but it is *not* spontaneous. Grace seeks you where you are.

2. *Grace accepts you as you are.* A wonderful old song of the faith expresses this well:

> Just as I am! without one plea
> But that Thy blood was shed for me,
> And that Thou bidd'st me come to Thee,
> O Lamb of God! I come! I come!

Grace says, "Come as you are." This is a strange concept to most people who think, *If there is a God at all, surely I can't come to Him the way I am.* That is the point of grace. Rahab was saved not because she gave up her harlotry, but rather because she asked to be saved. Now before you write a nasty letter to me about the need for believers to live holy lives, let me add another thought.

3. *Grace never leaves you where and as you are.* Grace says come as you are, but don't stay that way. It is grace that leads to repentance, not the other way around. You can't experience grace and look at sin the same. Grace will break the heart of the sinner. Then grace will transform the sinful heart.

Grace never leaves you where you are. Rahab did not give up her harlotry in order to experience grace. But the record clearly shows that, having experienced this undeserved grace, her life was never the same. The Bible is replete with accounts of throwaway people whose lives were never the same again, because they were recycled by grace.

Consider the story of Zaccheus (see Luke 19:1-10). You will remember the song from your childhood, "Zaccheus was a wee little man, and a wee little man was he." Zaccheus was the poster child for throwaway people. He was a tax collector, which has never been a popular profession; but in that day, it was considered a treasonous profession, full of thieves and traitors. But Jesus saw something more in Zaccheus and invited Himself into his home. Zaccheus was never the same. Suffice it to say, grace sought him where he was— accepted him as he was—but did not leave him where and as he was.

Look at the story of the Samaritan woman—married five times and living with a man who was not her legal husband (see John 4:1-42). You could have tattooed the word *throwaway* across her forehead. But follow her story, and you find that Jesus refused to treat her as a throwaway. She was recycled by grace.

Remember the story of the woman who was caught in the act of adultery (see John 8:1-11)? (Incidentally, I have always been puzzled by something. If they were able to catch the woman in the act, doesn't that imply that they caught the man as well? Where is the man?) Here was another throwaway waiting to be thrown away—until Jesus came along. I love what He said to her. "Neither do I condemn you; go and sin no more" (v. 11). That is grace—marvelous, wonderful, amazing grace! Grace seeks us where we are, accepts us as we are, but never leaves us where and as we are! But how does this work? Is it automatic? Do we have a part to play? Or do we just sit and wait for grace to do its thing?

Grace Initiates Faith

Everything begins with grace, but grace is not automatic. Grace initiates faith, but there comes a point in time when faith must respond to grace. A moment in time when you must do something about grace. Rahab did. After stating her belief in the one true God, Rahab takes action.

> "Now therefore, I beg you, swear to me by the Lord, since I have shown you kindness, that you also show kindness to my father's house, and give me a true token" (Joshua 2:12).

In this passage, Rahab has moved from the grace to believe, to a faith that acts. Here is a principle that needs to be understood. God offers grace, but He never imposes grace. There came a point in time when Rahab had to act upon that grace.

God had been working in her life. Grace had initiated faith. But suppose that's all that happened. Suppose that Rahab believed all the right things about the God of Israel but never acted on what she believed. Would she have been saved? She was told to hang a scarlet cord out the window and she would be spared. Suppose she believed, but never hung the cord out the window. Would she and her household have been spared? No!

Grace initiated faith; faith then responded to grace. Faith is active, not passive. Life-transforming faith is a verb, not a noun. You must choose . . . you must believe . . . you must claim . . . you must act. In Hebrews 11, the writer speaks of Rahab's salvation through faith:

> "By faith the walls of Jericho fell down after they were encircled for seven days. By faith the harlot Rahab did

not perish with those who did not believe, when she had received the spies with peace" (vv. 30, 31).

God's grace spared her through her faith, but it was not passive faith. James 2 describes her faith as a faith that took action:

> Likewise, was not Rahab the harlot also justified by works when she received the messengers and sent them out another way? For as the body without the spirit is dead, so faith without works is dead also (vv. 25, 26).

James presents an interesting scenario in what is considered one of the most controversial passages in the Bible. When Martin Luther read it, he wanted to rip it out. Luther assumed that James was espousing salvation based on works. Was Luther right? What does James mean? Simply this: Grace initiates faith, but there comes a point in time when faith has to respond to grace. You are saved by grace through faith, but it is a faith that works. Grace initiates faith; faith responds to grace. When faith responds to grace, grace and faith transform lives.

Several years ago, I was at a seminar. The leader asked each of us to share our testimony. We went around the room sharing and listening to the faith story of each person. It was an enjoyable, if somewhat predictable, exercise. Most of the testimonies could have been heard in any Sunday school class in America. That is, until the final man spoke. The leader had deliberately held him for last, and for good reason. His testimony absolutely blew us away.

He began with this statement: "Twenty years ago I was on death row. I had been convicted of a murder of which I truly was guilty." He went on to say, "I was a hardened criminal and had not only been sentenced to die, but my execution date was drawing near."

Needless to say, he had our attention. He continued, "There was a guard in that prison who was a Christian, and everyone knew it. I didn't like him and would have nothing to do with him. But in spite of my belligerence, he was always polite and pleasant to me. He would sing Christian songs, and when given an opportunity, he would talk about Christ. I could not stand the man, and I pushed him away."

He continued the story, "Within a few months of my execution date, one day this man walked into my cell, looked me right in the face and said, 'You know you are going to die. Have you even thought about your eternity?' I didn't want to hear it, and I demanded that he leave me alone."

"I was angry that he would be so bold. But after he left, I started thinking about his question. I was going to die, and I had not thought about eternity. Suddenly this truth penetrated my conscience. I wrestled all night with his question, until finally I came to the point that I had to talk to him. The next day, I asked him to come to my cell and tell me about his faith. In a simple way, he told me about Christ. There in that place I asked Jesus to be my Lord."

"The most remarkable thing happened," he said. "My sentence was overturned on appeal—not my conviction—just my sentence. I was no longer facing the death penalty. Shortly after that, I was offered parole." He added, "To this day, I don't know why they offered me parole, but they did, and I was released from prison. A few months earlier, I was facing execution, but now I was paroled and free. God was giving me a new life."

He could have ended the story right there. By this time, all of us were sitting in stunned silence, savoring the remarkable grace of God. But he was not finished, and what he shared next caught us all off guard. He closed his testimony by saying, "Today, I am a pastor of a church." Wow! Grace initiated faith, faith responded to grace, grace and faith transformed a life. Isn't that good? And if it happened to him, it can happen to you.

Don't think that the promised life is only for other people. If a prostitute can become the grandmother of a king and an ancestress of our Lord, just think of what God can do with you! The words of a hymn are so true:

> What a wonderful change
> In my life has been wrought,
> Since Jesus came into my heart!

Discussion Questions

1. Do you agree that grace initiates faith?

2. How would you explain the phrase "by grace through faith" to someone who had never heard the gospel before?

3. How does grace affect our lives in ways other than our salvation?

PART TWO

FIGHTING THE GOOD FIGHT

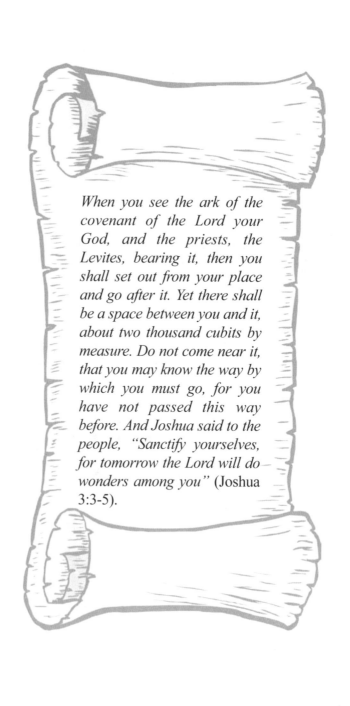

When you see the ark of the covenant of the Lord your God, and the priests, the Levites, bearing it, then you shall set out from your place and go after it. Yet there shall be a space between you and it, about two thousand cubits by measure. Do not come near it, that you may know the way by which you must go, for you have not passed this way before. And Joshua said to the people, "Sanctify yourselves, for tomorrow the Lord will do wonders among you" (Joshua 3:3-5).

6
The Art of Supernatural Living

Joshua 3

W hat have you experienced in your life that can only be explained by the supernaturalness of God? (I am not sure that *supernaturalness* is really a word, but I like the way it sounds, so I am going to say it again.) I repeat, What have you experienced in your life that can only be explained by the supernaturalness of God?

You may be one of those people who can honestly say your life is filled with the supernatural. As Adrian Rogers says, you might be "naturally supernatural." Your motto may be, "A miracle a day keeps the devil away." But if you are like many people, you are not sure you have ever truly experienced supernaturalness. What a pity . . . what a shame. I have already stated that the promised life is not a 24/7 life of supernaturalness, but I do believe that it is a life that knows the touch of the supernatural. Or stated more succinctly, there is a supernatural dimension to the promised life.

Joshua 3 begins the epic conquest of the Promised Land. From the outset, it was supernatural. Let me set the scene. The children of Israel were poised to cross into Canaan. Ahead of them was a formidable barrier—the mighty Jordan River. If you have been to that part of the world, you may snicker when I talk about the Jordan River as mighty and formidable. Ordinarily, it is anything *but* a raging torrent. Those who have never seen it often have the mistaken idea that the Jordan is a major tributary like the Mississippi. It is not. In fact, in my neck of the woods, we wouldn't call it a river. We would probably call it a creek and name a Baptist church after it. It isn't much of a river, as rivers go. In fact, at points you can wade across it.

But at this particular time, the Jordan River was at flood stage. "For the Jordan overflows all its banks during the whole time of harvest" (Joshua 3:15). The rains had come and the snows had melted on Mount Hermon, so the water was raging. I find it interesting that the Lord told them to move across at the worst possible time. God was testing them. They had a choice to make: Would they step out in faith, or play it safe? They stepped out in faith. The priests moved into the water carrying the ark of the covenant, and as they did, the water dried up for 60 miles—all the way to the city of Adam.

This is an incredible account—déjà vu of the Red Sea crossing. It is a story of God's people experiencing the dimension of the supernatural. To be sure, this is *not* the kind of thing that happens every day. But it did happen, and from it we can learn some powerful truths about the supernaturalness of the promised life.

Before we go further, I want to issue a disclaimer. This is going to be simple stuff, so simple it may offend your sophistication. But though it is simple, most people are not going to understand it. I doubt that one in 10 will "get it," because it deals with things supernatural. Writing to the Corinthians, the apostle Paul made it clear that some people simply are not equipped to perceive the supernatural. There are some Paul refers to as "natural" (see 1 Corinthians 2:14)—people who do not possess the Spirit of God in their lives and cannot discern spiritual (supernatural) things. But you can possess the Spirit of God and still not grasp the supernatural. If you are a Christian whose focus is always on the natural, you will have difficulty believing, accepting and experiencing something that is beyond the natural. Why bother with a passage that 90 percent of the people reading it will not fully understand? Because, if only 10 percent get it, it will revolutionize the church.

Believe in the Possibility

If you are to experience the supernatural dimension, you must believe in the possibility of supernatural living. Joshua clearly did.

"Sanctify yourselves, for tomorrow the Lord will do wonders among you" (Joshua 3:5). I like Joshua. He believed in the possibility of supernatural living. He believed in a God who "can." There are many, both outside the faith and within the faith, who do not believe that God can. The apostle Paul warned that this day would come. Speaking to Timothy, he made the following statement: "In the last days . . . [men will have] a form of godliness but denying its power. And from such people turn away" (2 Timothy 3:1, 5).

Please note that last phrase, "From such people turn away." The language means "run away." If you're around people who call themselves Christians, yet who do not believe in the supernaturalness of God, leave them alone. They are bad news. There are people who want us to believe that the miraculous, if it *ever* happened, is only a thing of the past. They would have us to believe that now, having the completed canon of Scripture, supernatural things don't happen—at least not as they happened in the past. Now we can read His Word and live under natural law.

Allow me to say a word about "natural" laws. There are none. There is no such thing as a "natural" law. In fact, there is no Mother Nature; there is only Father God. Therefore, there are no "laws of nature"—only laws of God. And if God made them, He can suspend them.

My family and I were on a vacation trip. The five of us were crowded into one small car. Every 30 minutes or so, somebody would need to stop. It didn't take long for that to get old and my patience to run thin. Finally, after one stop too many, I announced that I was making a new law: "No stopping until we are at least halfway there."

Thirty minutes later, we stopped again, only this time, nature was calling me. My kids were brutal. "What about the law? You laid down the law!" To which I replied, "I make the laws, I break the laws." I know what you are thinking—*That is very bad parenting.* You are right. But it is good theology. If God makes the laws, God can suspend the laws of nature. God is a supernatural God.

Just so you understand where I'm coming from and who I am, let me make it abundantly clear. I am a thoroughgoing supernaturalist. I don't just believe in a God who can—I believe in a God who will! I don't just believe in a God who once did—I believe in a God who still does!

I don't mean that I walk on water or call down fire

from heaven. I don't anoint handkerchiefs and send them out at $49.99, VISA and MasterCard accepted. But I do believe in a God who will enable you and me to live beyond the natural capacity of our lives.

Some time ago, I was listening to a broadcast of a high school football game. Playing on the defensive line was a young man who was too small for the position. He stood 5 feet 8 inches tall and weighed 150 pounds and was playing against two huge, offensive linemen, each weighing over 200 pounds. Evidently he was doing quite well. One of the commentators said, "You know, the little guy just plays bigger than himself." That young man was not playing by supernatural power; he was simply maximizing his natural capacity. But when I heard that statement, I remember thinking, *That is exactly the way we are supposed to live—bigger than ourselves. Life is supposed to be lived beyond natural capacity.*

If the truth were known, when it comes to the spiritual life, most of us don't even live up to the natural capacities that we possess. If we did, there is so much more we could do. But God designed us not to live beneath, or even within, but *beyond* our capacities. God designed us to be people of faith who live boldly and trust God for the results. A.W. Tozer said, "God is looking for people through whom He can do the impossible. What a pity that we plan only the things we can do by ourselves."

The apostle Paul wrote, "I can do all things through Christ who strengthens me" (Philippians 4:13). It is not a can-do attitude we're talking about. It is a God-can-do attitude. If you want to experience the supernatural dimension, you must believe in the possibility of supernatural living.

Go With God

Believing in the possibility is not enough. If you want to experience the supernatural dimension, you must place yourself in the flow of what God is doing. Joshua told the people to watch the ark and follow after it. What was the ark of the covenant? What did it mean to the people?

The ark was actually a furnishing from the Holy of Holies in the Tabernacle. It was a wooden chest overlaid with gold. It measured approximately 2 feet by 4 feet. Inside the ark was the Book of the Law, the tablets with the Commandments upon them, Aaron's rod that budded in the wilderness, and a gold pot containing some of the manna that had fallen from heaven.

Incidentally, we do not know what happened to the ark of the covenant. There are many legends and myths concerning it, and scholars are divided. Some believe it was stolen in 950 B.C. by foreign invaders. Others believe Nebuchadnezzar destroyed it in 586 B.C., along with some of the utensils in the Temple. One theory holds that the ark of the covenant is buried deep within the western wall of the Temple mount in a secret chamber that no one knows about anymore. Many people in Israel believe the day will come when the Temple will be rebuilt and in the process, the ark will be recovered.

The ark of the covenant represented the presence of God in their midst. It served as the visible reminder of the invisible God with them. It was there that the Shekinah (or presence of God) dwelled. Now you can understand Joshua's instruction, "Watch the ark, and wherever the ark goes, you go." Wherever God is going, we must go with Him.

There is a principle here that most of us miss. Good

people will sometimes say, "I've been a Christian for years, and I have never experienced the supernatural." The problem is they are not looking for the hand of God, so they never see it.

Let me dispel a myth. There is the idea that when we become Christians, God joins Himself to our life, and we can exercise His power as we see fit. We seem to think God wants to join in our plan. People will say, "God is on our side." I have heard people pray before a volley-ball game and ask God to "be on their side." Let's get it straight. God doesn't join us. God allows us to join *Him*. We don't do our thing in His power. That is backward. Here is a revelation: *God is not on your side.* He is not on anybody's side. God *is* the side! Be very careful when you pray. Do not ask God to be on your side. Instead pray, "Dear God, help me to be on Your side." Joshua was saying, "Go after God." How does this work? Let me put this in practical terms.

1. *Pay attention to what God is doing in your community.* Henry Blackaby says it well: "If you see God doing something, drop everything and get in on it." Go with God. I am not encouraging church hopping to find the best show in town. But I am saying when God is doing something in your community, don't let your loyalty to a dead church keep you from a living work of God.

2. *Pay attention to what God is doing in your church.* What is God anointing and blessing? What kind of worship does God seem to be blessing? Move in that direction. What ministries does God seem to be anointing these days? Move in that direction.

3. *Pay attention to what God may be doing in your home.* Do you want a touch of the supernatural in your marriage? I have a suggestion for you: Pay attention to

87

what God is doing in your spouse's life, and go in that direction. There are marriages on the rocks for this very reason. God is doing something in the husband or the wife, and the other is not paying attention. I have known wives whose husbands are struggling as God does a new work in them, but they fail to see God's hand in it. Many a man in the throes of a mid-life crisis is like Jacob wrestling with God. Some wives are not in tune with God, or their husband, enough to sense what is happening. The same goes for husbands who never sense what God is doing in their wives. What is God doing in your mate? Don't fight it. Join it, and see what God will do in your home.

What is God doing in the lives of your children? What are the gifts God is developing in them? What is the natural inclination God has given them? Watch for it, and then get in on it. Rather than trying to shape that child in your image, let that child grow up in God's image—the image that God has put in his or her life.

4. *Pay attention to what God is doing in your sphere of influence.* What is God doing at your office among your coworkers and friends? Do you want to be an effective witness? Pay attention to what God is doing, and get in on it. Go in that direction. The idea is this: God is *always* doing something. There is never a time when He is not. Pay attention, and put yourself in the flow of what God's doing.

5. *Pay attention to what God is doing in your life.* What things are changing around you and in you? I find that most people are aware that things are constantly changing in them and around them, but they never seem to pick up on the idea that God is doing a new work in their life. In my own life, there are areas of ministry I no

longer feel God blessing as He once did. But there are new areas of ministry that He seems to be opening to me. Could God be changing me? Do I just keep doing what I have always done, or do I move in the new direction God seems to be blessing? Go with the flow of God, not against it, if you want to see the supernatural dimension of the promised life.

One last word: Stay in the flow. It is important that you not lose sight of where God is going next. There is a strange caveat to Joshua's instruction. In Joshua 3:4, the people are told to follow the ark, but not too closely: "Yet there shall be a space between you and it, about two thousand cubits by measure."

Two thousand cubits is roughly half a mile. They are to follow after the ark, but they are to maintain a half-mile radius around it. Why? Verse 4 continues and gives us the rationale. "Do not come near it, that you may know the way by which you must go, for you have not passed this way before."

The idea is simple. Don't get so close to it that you obscure the view. Make sure it is kept out front, so the people can keep their focus on it at all times. If you ever lose focus on where God's going, you are in trouble.

How does that apply? Follow God, and don't lose track of what God is doing now. Don't lose focus. There are whole generations that have done just that. They have lost the focus of what God is doing now. In a previous generation, we discerned where God was going and followed, but if we are not careful, we will lose our focus on what God is doing now. Following God is not a one-time affair; it is a day-by-day thing. Where is God going now? The constant prayer of every believer must be, "What next, Lord? What next, Lord?" That is the only way we will continue in the supernatural dimension of the promised life.

Discussion Questions

1. Do you believe in the possibility of supernatural living, and to what extent is your life affected by your belief?

2. What does God seem to be anointing in your community or church?

3. What does God seem to be doing in your home or in your life?

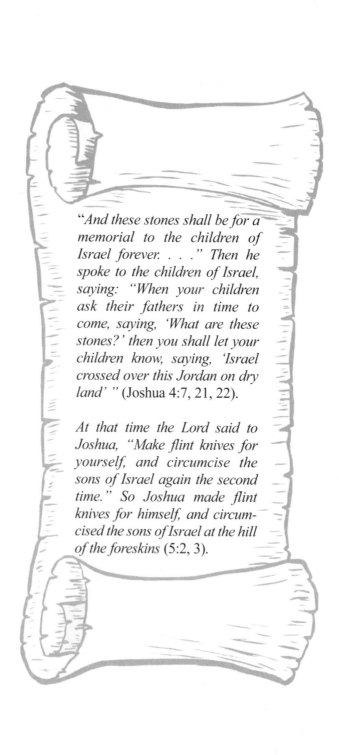

"And these stones shall be for a memorial to the children of Israel forever. . . ." Then he spoke to the children of Israel, saying: "When your children ask their fathers in time to come, saying, 'What are these stones?' then you shall let your children know, saying, 'Israel crossed over this Jordan on dry land' " (Joshua 4:7, 21, 22).

At that time the Lord said to Joshua, "Make flint knives for yourself, and circumcise the sons of Israel again the second time." So Joshua made flint knives for himself, and circumcised the sons of Israel at the hill of the foreskins (5:2, 3).

7

Pass It On

It was an unusually nice day. I, along with 10 others, was attending a doctoral seminar in Louisville, Kentucky. It was no secret that most of us would rather have been outside enjoying the sunshine. The summer Olympics was to be held in Atlanta that year, and the Olympic flame was scheduled to pass through Louisville that day. It just so happened, it was to pass on the street directly in front of our building. In an uncharacteristic moment of mercy, the professor suggested we break from class and watch the exchange of the torch.

We made our way to the street, already crowded with spectators. After about 30 minutes of waiting, the flame came into sight. Running up the road was an elderly man. I am not good at ages, but I guessed him to be in his late 60s to early 70s. He was barely able to hold the torch with both hands. I said he was running, but he wasn't really. He was actually shuffling. He shuffled past me about 10 yards and handed the torch off to a little boy who was about 10 or 12 years of age. It was an impressive sight: a member of the oldest generation passing the flame to a member of the youngest generation. I remember thinking, *What a great picture that is.* That is the way faith is supposed to be passed—from one generation to the next.

This promised life God has for you is also for your children. Speaking of the promise of the Holy Spirit, Peter said, "The promise is to you and to your children" (Acts 2:39). Unfortunately, we have come to a time when the faith is not being passed on. Consider this startling fact: In our culture, 80 to 85 percent of the oldest generation have affiliated with the Christian faith. Those of you who are 65 and older can't think of anyone in your high school class who has not. I don't mean that they were all dynamic Christians, but they were at least affiliated with the faith.

But the alarming reality is that the generation born after 1976 is *not* in the faith. Some studies show that less than 15 percent are actively affiliating with the faith. And statistics repeatedly show that after the age of 20, the odds go down—not up—that these unbelievers will ever become believers in Christ. That means in our youngest generation, most are not, and will not be, in the faith.

We blame everyone else for this. We blame the media, the culture, the schools. But the truth is, we now have a generation of believers who are not passing on their faith—a generation that seems more concerned with developing soccer skills in their children than passing on their spiritual heritage. This brings us to the question: How do we pass on the faith?

Joshua 4—5 gives us insight. These two chapters are about one generation making sure that the next generation knows the truth. The children of Israel have passed over the Jordan. When they get to the other side, two peculiar events occur. First, Joshua selects 12 strong men to take 12 large stones out of the dried-up riverbed, and erects them in Gilgal as a memorial.

Then in chapter 5, God tells Joshua to take flint knives and circumcise all the males that have been born in the wilderness. The men who came out of Egypt into the wilderness had been circumcised. These had not. What is the significance of these accounts? These two events are designed to pass on the faith.

Create a Faith-Enriched Environment

How do you pass on the faith? You must create a faith-enriched environment—an environment where your kids will develop a natural hunger for the faith. In Joshua 4, the people are told to take the stones and pile them up so that their children will see them and ask what the stones mean. And when the children asked, the Israelites were to respond with the story of how God intervened in the life of their nation by drying up the river so they could cross. They were creating what I call a faith-enriched environment.

This is needed more today than ever. We live in a culture that is anything but faith-enriched. Many of us grew up at a time when the culture encouraged faith, but that day is gone.

Dr. Elmer Towns was speaking to a group of pastors. After he spoke, a young pastor asked, "Dr. Towns, what do you consider to be the most critical issue facing the church in the 21st century?" Dr. Towns did not hesitate. "The most critical issue is the Biblical and spiritual illiteracy of the younger generation." He went on to say, "For the first time in the history of American Christianity, we are producing a generation that knows not God." I think he is right.

When I was growing up, if you were the child of non-Christian parents, you would still be exposed to Judeo-Christian values. At the very least, the Ten Commandments were on the walls of school classrooms. You heard prayer and Bible reading in school. The culture was "Judeo-Christian friendly." That is no longer true. For the first time in our history, it is entirely possible for a child to go all the way through the public education system, from kindergarten to Ph.D., and never once seriously encounter the Judeo-Christian value system, let alone the gospel of Christ. Even in the Bible Belt, we have become Biblically illiterate. That is why it's so important to create a faith-enriched environment in our homes.

Two things are required to accomplish this, and they are rather simple. First is visual stimulation. Your kids need to see things that spark curiosity for the faith. Joshua 4 is about 12 large rocks. Those rocks served as a visual stimulation to cause the children to ask, "What does this mean?" A faith-enriched environment will have things that cause your children to ask, "What does this mean?"

I have discovered something about human nature. Whatever is important to us we will put on display. What is on display in your home? If you go into the home of grandparents, you will see pictures of grandkids. Why? Because grandkids are important to grandparents. If you go into the home of an athlete, you may see trophies and reminders of past athletic achievement. If you go into the home of a fisherman, you will see stuffed dead fish hanging on the wall.

What is important to you? Shouldn't the home of a Christian have something that speaks of faith? What kind of pictures or plaques do you have on the wall? What kind of magazines do you have on the coffee table? What kind of books do you have on your bookshelves? What kind of music plays in your house? Rock and roll? Country? I like them all. I am not saying that you can't have different types, but isn't it reasonable that Christian music should be dominant in a Christian home? Create a faith-enriched environment in your home by providing visual stimulation.

A faith-enriched environment also requires verbal confirmation. Talk about your faith. Your children should hear about the faith from *your* lips. Joshua told the people, "When your children see these memorials stones and ask, then you tell them—*you* tell them" (see 4:21, 22).

In Joel 1, the people of faith are instructed, "Tell it to your children, and let your children tell it to their children, and their children to the next generation" (v. 3, *NIV*). In Deuteronomy 6, Moses said, "You shall teach them diligently to your children, and shall talk of them when you sit in your house, when you walk by the way, when you lie down, and when you rise up" (v. 7).

If your children do not hear about the faith from you, they may not hear about the faith at all. In this culture, they are more likely to hear about gay and lesbian rights than they are about Judeo-Christian values. Your kids need to hear what *you* believe. Consider these questions:

- Do your kids know your testimony?

- Have they heard your testimony of faith enough to retell it at your funeral?

Create a faith-enriched environment by talking about the faith. But a faith-enriched environment is not enough.

Provide a Faith Example

We must provide what I call a faith-specific example. In Joshua 5, we have an odd story. Except for the last few verses, this chapter recounts a very bloody, painful act of commitment—a covenant act. No sooner had they crossed the Jordan River than Joshua was told to take flint knives and circumcise all the males who had been born in the wilderness. Keep in mind, they were facing an enemy when they crossed over, yet they conducted a mass circumcision. I will spare you the details, except to say this was a powerful event. This was a faith-specific example of their commitment, and it was a big commitment. Words are important, but deeds matter most. Your kids need a faith-enriched environment, but more than anything else, they need a faith-specific example of your commitment.

In the simplest terms, your kids need to see your conviction. When these 40,000 men submitted themselves to the procedure of circumcision, they were saying, "We mean business with God."

This is where we often fall short. It's easy to talk about the faith, but it is another matter to live it. Words are cheap if they aren't backed by conviction. I am convinced this is the reason so many children of church members don't follow Christ. They hear confession without seeing the conviction. Even simple acts of conviction make a great impact. Something as simple as taking your children to church can make a huge difference. Notice I said *take* your kids to church, not *send* them. Your kids are not dumb—they know whether or not your faith matters to you.

I was speaking to a man not long ago who made this statement, "Pastor, I don't come to church every Sunday, and I don't insist on my children being there." When I asked why not, he said, "Because I don't want them to hate the church. My parents made me go to every service, and I hated it." When I asked him, "Did your father attend with you when you were a child?" he looked at me as if I had lost my mind and said, "No, of course not." I suspect his parents *making* him attend is not what caused him to hate church. Rather, it is the fact that they sent him *alone*. There was no faith-specific example.

Your kids need to see that your faith matters to you, not just by the public display of faith. A private example is needed as well. The way your faith is lived out at home matters much. Don't misunderstand what I'm saying. I'm not suggesting that you make your home into a religious boot camp. Occasionally, people do exactly that, and create a miserable existence for their children.

Frankly, I think home ought to be a place of fun—a place where your kids see you as genuine. It should be a place of laughter, a good-time place, a place your kids enjoy. To be sure, they won't always appreciate the way you act. But don't let that stop you.

A number of years ago, my wife and I had one of those moments that endear you to your children—an experience we have remembered often over the years. It was one of those rare occasions, when all three of our kids were not under our feet, but in another part of the house. I went into the kitchen and found my wife at the sink washing dishes. I looked at her, and she looked at me, and I thought, *She needs to be kissed.* Sweeping her into my arms, I kissed her and held her tight, for fear she may swoon. (I am, after all, a very good kisser.) About a minute and a half into the kiss, I heard the pitter-patter of little feet. Not breaking the kiss, I opened one eye and looked down. Standing next to us was our 3-year-old daughter, Jennifer.

My first thought was, *I'd better stop doing this, before she gets the wrong idea.* But then I thought, *No, I'm not going to stop, because I want her to get the right idea. I want her to know that Mommy and Daddy are real people who love one another.* So we continued to kiss. A few moments passed, and we heard her clear her throat several times in an exaggerated manner. A moment later, I felt her tug on my pants leg. Finally, we broke the kiss and looked down. As we did, Jennifer looked up at us with her big eyes gleaming and said, "You people are sick."

Your kids will not always appreciate your being genuine, but don't let that stop you. Be fun at home. Be genuine. Let your faith inform the way you live. Make your home not just a place of fun—make it a place of faith. Let your kids see your patience, hear your prayers and watch as you read your Bible. Let your children see Mom and Dad having a quiet time. Let them see what it means to live the Christian faith.

The bottom line is this: Every generation has the responsibility of passing the faith on to the next generation. And faith is caught more than it is taught. Let me tell you why this matters so much. You no doubt have heard the old saying, "You can't take it with you when you're gone." The idea is that when you die, you leave everything behind; nothing in this life transcends eternity. That is not necessarily true.

There is one thing God has given that we can have with us in heaven—the souls of those we love, whom God has entrusted to us. The only thing God ever gave you that will transcend time into eternity are the souls of your children, if your faith in Christ becomes their faith in Christ. Pass it on!

Discussion Questions

1. Do you agree that parents today are less focused on their children's spiritual development than in times past? If so, why?

2. In what ways have you sought to create a faith-enriched environment in your home?

3. What are the faith examples you have seen in the lives of others that have shaped your own faith the most?

And the Lord said to Joshua: "See! I have given Jericho into your hand, its king, and the mighty men of valor" (Joshua 6:2).

8

The Jericho Factor

Two steps forward and one step back. That has been the description of my spiritual life at its best over the years. I suppose it could be worse. It could be one step forward and two steps back. The truth is I have never found the promised life to be smooth sailing. About the time I begin to make significant progress, something happens—an obstacle arises . . . an unexpected problem occurs . . . an old habit will crop up. This is what I call "the Jericho factor." Simply stated, we have an enemy: Satan, the devil, the Evil One. Call him what you will, but be assured he will not let you go into the promised life unchallenged.

Most believers come to understand this over time simply by trial and error. You may have heard someone say, "Things are going so well. I wonder what is about to happen?" Why do we say things like this? Because by experience, we have learned that when things are going well, something always happens. A "Jericho" is always on the horizon.

Joshua 6 is the story of progress interrupted. The children of Israel have crossed over the Jordan and are now

103

camped at a place called Gilgal. Facing them is a formidable obstacle—the mighty fortress of Jericho.

Jericho was indeed formidable. The oldest, continuous city in the world, Jericho was considered to be an impregnable fortress, the most heavily fortified site outside of Egypt.

To understand this story, you must know something of the geopolitical dynamics at work. Jericho sat in a strategic location. To the north was the trade route leading up to the valley of the Galilee. To the east were the trade routes over the mountains leading to Jerusalem and Hebron. Guarding these trade routes was the fortress of Jericho. To not deal with this city would threaten, or maybe stop, the progress of the entire nation. The Promised Land could not be taken until Jericho fell.

"Jerichos" are universal; all of us have them. If we don't overcome them, we will never have the life God intends. Perhaps your Jericho is internal, a chronic issue within. You are afraid, or you lack faith. Perhaps it is a sense of insecurity that crops up in your life that, in time, becomes a chronic problem for you. It could be a temptation to sin that has thrown you back time and time again.

Maybe your Jericho is external. There may be someone who is pulling you down spiritually. I do not know what your Jericho is, but I am quite sure you have one. I have experienced the Jericho factor many times in my life. There are things that, if I let them, would keep me from the life God has promised. Claiming what is rightfully mine and yours will require that we deal with the Jerichos that will come our way.

How do we deal with the Jerichos of life? At this point, it is tempting to spout simple formulas and platitudes, but

I am not going to do that. I have discovered that life does not respond well to neat formulas. I've tried them, and they don't work. What I need are simple truths to guide me. That is what you have in this story. The story of Jericho reveals several simple truths.

A Strengthening Presence

Jerichos are scary. Thank God, we do not have to face them alone. This will sound familiar. I have discovered in my own life that though the Lord is always with me, there is a special sense of His presence in Jericho moments. Joshua made this discovery.

> And it came to pass, when Joshua was by Jericho, that he lifted his eyes and looked, and behold, a Man stood opposite him with His sword drawn in His hand. And Joshua went to Him and said to Him, "Are you for us or for our adversaries?" So He said, "No, but as Commander of the army of the Lord I have now come" (5:13, 14).

This was the first big test of Joshua's leadership. No doubt, he was feeling the pressure. As he looked out at Jericho looming before him, Joshua sensed a presence. He turned and there stood a man with a sword in hand. Startled, Joshua asks, "Who are you? Are you for us, or are you against us? Are you friend, or are you foe?" The man answered, "I am the commander of the army of the Lord."

Who was this person? Some suggest that it was an angel, but this was no angel. Joshua fell down and worshiped him. Angels never receive worship. The Lord alone is worthy to be worshiped. This is none other than the Lord himself.

Bible scholars believe this to be one of several preincarnate manifestations of Christ we find in the Bible. Jesus did not just come on the scene 2,000 years ago. The Bible tells us He was from the very beginning. "In the beginning was the Word, and the Word was with God, and the Word was God" (John 1:1). In Joshua 1, we are told that the Lord spoke to Joshua, but we have no record that the Lord appeared to him. Now Joshua experienced Him in a unique way.

I have never seen the Lord like this, but I will tell you that there is never a time when He is more real to me than in those Jericho moments of my life—those times when I face obstacles that could potentially derail my faith. I don't know that His presence is greater at those moments, but I do know that at those times, I have a keen awareness of His presence. And I know like Joshua, I am *not* alone, and neither are you.

There is an interesting side note to this passage. This was not an angel, but angels were there. Did you notice the phrase "the Commander of the army of the Lord"? What is the army of the Lord? He is talking about the angels. Do you believe in angels? I hope you do. I don't know how anyone who professes to be a believer could believe otherwise. The Bible is replete with the account of angels. The life and ministry of our Lord was surrounded by angels. Angels appeared at Christ's birth, death, resurrection and ascension. And angels will come with Him when He returns. I personally believe guardian angels make up the hedge of protection God places around His people.

One of my favorite stories in Scripture is the story of Elisha's servant. He was afraid because the Assyrians were poised to attack. Elisha prayed that the Lord would open his (spiritual) eyes, that he might see. The Lord granted the request. When he looked around, on the mountains surrounding them were thousands, if not millions, of angels. Ooh, I like that! I like the idea of angels all around me.

The Book of Hebrews tells us that angels are ministering spirits that minister unto the saints. That's us. Isn't that fantastic? I am never alone. No matter what the Jericho might be, I am never alone. When I get discouraged or weak in the Lord's work, I visualize in my own mind the Lord in me and the angels around me. Now this is ground we have already covered, but it does not hurt for us to be reminded. We are never, no not ever, no never ever ever alone!

A Strange Strategy

The presence of the Lord was a great encouragement to Joshua. He was anxious to hear the Lord's strategy for defeating Jericho. I can almost see him with quill in hand, ready to jot down the plan. "What shall I do, Lord? Where shall I attack?" Joshua was ready to do the Lord's bidding. But he had no idea what the Lord would bid him do. The Lord spoke:

> "You shall march around the city, all you men of war; you shall go all around the city once. This you shall do six days. And seven priests shall bear seven trumpets of rams' horns before the ark. But the seventh day you shall march around the city seven times, and the priests shall blow the trumpets. It shall come to pass, when they make a long blast with the ram's horn, and when you hear the sound of the trumpet, that all the people shall

shout with a great shout; then the wall of the city will fall down flat" (Joshua 6:3-5).

What a strange strategy. How absurd this must have sounded to the officers when Joshua reported back. But Joshua did not discount it. It was God's strategy.

Our God is no stranger to strange strategies. Remember the story of Noah and the Flood? The earth was a stench in the nostrils of God; the sins of men had risen up before Him, and God said, "I'm going to fix this." So He sends a flood. That was a strange strategy.

Remember the story of Gideon? Gideon was called "[God's] mighty man of valor" (Judges 6:12). He was anything but. The Lord had a monumental assignment for him: Destroy the Midianites. The Midianites were over 100,000 strong. Gideon sent out a call to arms and 32,000 men responded. He was still outnumbered three to one, but at least he felt better about the odds. But then God spoke! To paraphrase, He said, "You have 31,700 men too many. Keep only 300 men, and send the rest home" (see Judges 7:1-8). That was a strange strategy. The more things change, the more they stay the same. God is still the God of strange strategies. Let me list a few examples:

- A young woman's husband is not a believer. She is so frustrated with him. How does she deal with him? Peter says she is to love him submissively and yield her life to him (see 1 Peter 3:1, 2). What a strange strategy.

- A man has a wife who does not live up to his expectations. How does he treat her? Ephesians 5:25 says he is to love her as Christ loved the church . . . a strange strategy.

- Perhaps you find yourself in a job situation you don't particularly like; you are looking for work that fits you better. What should you do until you find another one? Paul says you work as if you're working for the Lord (see Colossians 3:23) . . . another strange strategy.

- Do you have an enemy, someone who is putting you down? How do you handle her? The Scripture says you heap coals of kindness on her head (see Proverbs 25:21, 22; Romans 12:20). This is a strange strategy indeed!

God is a God of strange strategies; don't discount them. Most Jerichos are conquered by strange strategies. Seek to do things God's way, and don't give up. Perhaps you have been following a strange strategy that does not seem to be working. Don't stop short. When it comes to Jericho, endurance is often the key to victory.

Remember the strategy God gave Joshua. He told him to have the people march around the city once a day for six days, and seven times on the seventh day. If I have done the math correctly, that is 13 times around. Why would God require this? He could speak a word, and the walls would come down. There have been many theories over the years as to why they had to march around 13 times. One scholar suggested that this was done to unnerve the people of Jericho. The sight of all these people marching would surely put the fear of God in them.

Another scholar suggested that they marched around the city 13 times to destabilize the walls. According to this theory, all that marching created seismic activity under Jericho and on the seventh time around on the seventh day, all the people in Jericho would have been on the wall, curious to see what was going to happen. The accumulated weight of all those Canaanites—plus the seismic activity of 2 million people marching around—would cause the city to fall.

Coming Up Short

I don't think they marched around 13 times to unnerve the people of Jericho or to destabilize the walls of the fortress. I suspect God had them march around 13 times to test the children of Israel, to see if they would follow through. I can think of no other reason.

Suppose they had marched around the city one time a day for six days and six times on the seventh day, but had not marched around the city the seventh time on the seventh day. What would have happened? Nothing. They could have shouted until their voices were hoarse, but nothing would have happened. Coming up short is a real temptation. It happens all the time.

I see this in marriages. Couples pledge their faith one to the other "until death do us part." Then they realize, *This is harder than we thought.* "For better or for worse" is worse than they thought. They come up short. Endurance is the key to victory; don't stop short. How does this work?

A man worked in the same place for years—the only Christian on the job. The workplace is a profane environment, and he finds living out the faith to be tough. But he believes God is with him. In fact, he consciously practices the presence of God. His lifestyle seems strange to his coworkers. Ostracized and ridiculed for his faith, he does not give up. He does not give in. He endures over time. When everyone else is yielding to temptation, he remains strong.

Then it happens. One day a coworker comes to him, devastated with the news that his wife has left him. He doesn't know where to turn or what to say. He finds the one man in the place whose life seems to be different. With a broken spirit he asks, "Can you help me?" In case you missed it, let me tell you what has happened. *A wall just fell in Jericho.* This man is poised to claim a soul for Christ.

A woman's husband, who is not a believer, has caused her grief for years. As time has gone by, he has not been kind about her faith. Yet, she endures. She continues to seek God's presence in her home. With God's help, she commits herself to being the wife she should be. She does not give up. Then it happens. One day, she comes home to find him sitting in the living room with the lights off. There are tears in his eyes. She has never seen him cry. Startled, she asks, "Honey, what's wrong?" He replies with a shaky voice, "I don't know. I just don't know. My life is a mess. Can you help me? What should I do?" In case you missed it, let me tell you what has happened. *A wall just fell in Jericho.* She is poised to claim a soul for Christ.

Two parents have done the very best they know how to do for their child. In spite of it all, she becomes a rebellious young woman. She breaks their hearts time and time again. They believe God is with them and will be with her. They do not give up. They love her unconditionally. Though they have not seen her in months and don't even know where she is, they pray for her every day. Then it happens. The phone rings in the middle of the night. He answers, only to hear these words: "Daddy,

I've made a mess out of my life. Will you help me? Can I come home?" In case you missed it, let me tell you what has happened. *A wall just fell in Jericho.* They are poised to claim a soul for Christ.

That is how it works if you don't quit. Endurance is the key. Everyone is going to face a Jericho. It's just a matter of time. When it happens to you, remember you're not alone. There is a way to face it. Though it may seem strange, follow God's strategy. If you'll just be faithful and not quit, you will overcome. I promise you, the wall *will* fall.

Discussion Questions

1. What are the "Jerichos" that consistently threaten your spiritual progress?

2. Have you ever discerned God leading you to follow a strange strategy that other people would not understand?

3. Can you recall an occasion when endurance brought victory in your life?

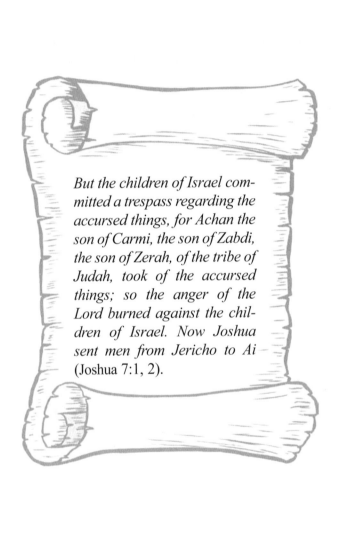

But the children of Israel committed a trespass regarding the accursed things, for Achan the son of Carmi, the son of Zabdi, the son of Zerah, of the tribe of Judah, took of the accursed things; so the anger of the Lord burned against the children of Israel. Now Joshua sent men from Jericho to Ai (Joshua 7:1, 2).

9

This Thing Called Sin

W hatever happened to old-fashioned moral decency? The rage these days is reality TV. Am I the only one, or does anybody else think that reality TV is just raunchy TV? Did the Ten Commandments suddenly expire and no one let me know?

At the age of 80, Karl Menninger, the world-renowned mental health worker and founder of the Menninger Clinic, wrote a book titled *Whatever Became of Sin?* Good question. It would seem that we need a wake-up call concerning this thing called *sin*. We need a reality check. Joshua 7 is just that—a wake-up call, a reality check.

In the last chapter, we witnessed the fall of Jericho, unquestionably one of the most unusual military victories in human history. Immediately after the fall of Jericho, the children of Israel went to battle again, this time with a tiny little village no larger than its name, Ai. Unfortunately, their military strategists did not take Ai seriously. The result was catastrophic. Mighty Israel, who defeated Jericho, is forced to turn and run from tiny Ai. Tragically, 36 of their fighting men are killed.

When word reached Joshua about the battle, he fell on his face and cried out, "God, why? Why? Why have You let this happen?" The Lord responded by saying, "Joshua, get up off your face. There is sin in the camp" (see 7:7-10). To understand the story, we must go back to the Lord's instruction concerning Jericho. In chapter 6, Joshua was told to instruct the people to touch nothing in Jericho. They were to take nothing for themselves. To the victor goes the spoil, and the victory was the Lord's; therefore, the booty of battle belonged to Him. But Achan willfully disregarded the warning. He removed 200 shekels of silver, a wedge of gold and a beautiful Babylonian garment. Achan then took his loot to his tent and buried it. Achan had sinned, and because of that sin, all of Israel suffered.

This is an interesting story, but what is its significance to us? It serves as a reality check concerning sin. Claiming the promised life that is rightfully ours requires that we deal with this thing called *sin*.

All Sin Has a Consequence

Reality check: *No sin is inconsequential.* Sin is no big deal, right? After all, what can it hurt? No doubt Achan is thinking, *If I do this thing, it won't hurt me.* He digs a hole in the ground under his tent and buries his stash, thinking, *Nobody will know; nobody will ever be the wiser.* Achan could have dug all the way to China and not adequately hidden his sin, because God's Word says, "Be sure your sin will find you out" (Numbers 32:23). "There is nothing covered that will not be revealed, and hidden that will not be made known" (Matthew 10:26). And every sin has a consequence.

Incidentally, the consequence is not just to you. Because Achan sinned, all Israel suffered and his family was destroyed. What are the consequences of sin?

1. *Sin will humble you.* Your sin will find you out, and when it does, you will be humbled.

Life in itself is humbling enough. Have you ever been humbled by life? If you haven't been yet, sooner or later you will be, because life has a way of knocking you on your backside.

One of my most humbling moments came as a freshman in high school. I was the youngest member of our junior varsity team, barely 13 years of age. Along with three other players, I was chosen to dress out with the varsity team for a game. Even better, I was told that if things went well, I might get in the game. I was so proud. I told every girl I knew.

It was the third game of the season, and things were going quite well. We were so far ahead, the coaches thought it safe to put the freshmen in. I was sent out on the kickoff team. Now anybody who knows anything about football knows that the kickoff team is reserved for freshmen and fools. It is suicide duty. But I didn't care. I went strutting out to my position. The ball was kicked, and I ran down the field. This was going to be my moment—my brief shining moment. I was determined to make the tackle and then bask in my own glory.

Everything was going according to plan, until suddenly, I tripped and fell flat on my face. That was bad enough. But what made matters worse—I realized I had tripped on my own pants! As I was running down the field, my hip pads had come loose, causing my pants to fall to my ankles. My definition of a humbling experience is being a 13-year-old freshman, lying facedown in front of thousands of people, with my bare posterior stuck up in the air.

I repeat, life has a way of humbling you. If you haven't figured that out, you will. But if life humbles you, what will sin do?

- Many whose names were once revered are no longer revered because of sin.

- Churches are humbled by the sin of its members.

- Wives are humiliated and humbled by the sin of their husbands.

- Husbands are humbled by the sin of their wives.

- Parents are humbled by the sin of the children.

Your sin will find you out, and when it does, it will humble you *and* those around you.

2. *Sin will do more than humble you—it will ruin you.* The name *Ai* means "ruins." And Ai was almost Israel's ruin. Sin will ruin a marriage, destroy a life and devastate a church. The person who says sin is no big deal will find out that it is. One act of rebellion can, and often has, ruined an otherwise promising life. If you sin, you will suffer. All sin carries a price. There are no inconsequential sins.

No Exceptions to the Rule

Reality check: *You are not the exception to the rule.* Achan thought he was. Achan is an enigma. Though not a pagan, he acts as one. He knowingly transgressed the will of the God in whom he said he believes. How did that happen? There are only two possibilities.

The first is *ignorance.* Achan could claim that he was simply unaware. He would not be alone. I have known many people over the years who claimed ignorance when it comes to sin. And in some cases, it is the truth. In this day of Biblical illiteracy, many people are simply ignorant. On occasion, I have dealt with couples living together without marriage. When we talk about the moral consequences and realities of that arrangement, they will look at me with a stunned expression on their face and say, "We did not know." People today truly do not know.

Achan's problem, however, clearly was not ignorance. That leaves us with only one other possibility: arrogance. *Arrogance* is thinking that you are the exception to the rule.

Does that sound familiar? It should, because we are all guilty of this to some degree. Our natural tendency is to assume that, though something may be wrong for everyone else, we are the exception to the rule. Frankly, I have never known anyone to do something wrong who did not think at the time that it was the right thing for them to do.

We human beings are remarkable in our ability to rationalize behavior. Two teenagers in the backseat of a car . . . a businessman cheating on his taxes . . . a corrupt politician . . . an adulterous wife . . . a cheating husband—all think they are the exception to the rule.

If I said to you that I have heard every excuse, that would not be true. There are as many excuses as there are sins. But I have heard my share of them. Here are a few:

- "But I love him."

- "The government takes so much of my money. I don't think it is cheating."

- "If my boss had paid me what I'm really worth, I would never have done what I did."

- "If you had to live with the wife I live with, you'd cheat on her too."

I can almost hear Achan saying, "Who is Joshua to tell me what I can and cannot do? I've been in this wilderness for 40 years, and I have nothing to show for it. I have a wife to keep happy and kids to clothe."

I counseled a man who had decided to leave his wife. He was already having an affair with another woman. When I asked, "Don't you know what you're doing is wrong?" His response was, "I have prayed about it. And I have come to believe God wants me to be happy." In other words, "I am the exception to the rule." Let me make this very clear: *Achan* was not the exception to the rule. *I* am not the exception to the rule. *You* are not the exception to the rule. If you sin, you suffer. *There are no exceptions to the rule.*

She was 19 years old, a beautiful coed at Tulane University. At the insistence of her mother, she came to my office. With a rather smug attitude, she recited an entire litany of sins: the men she had slept with, the drugs she was currently taking, the parties she had recently attended. This went on for quite some time, until finally she said, "And I don't have to feel guilty about any of this."

Being more than a little concerned, I asked, "Why shouldn't you feel guilty?" to which she replied, "Because my therapist tells me that I am a product of my environment and not responsible for my behavior; therefore, I need not feel guilty."

Not knowing what to say to her at that point, I just stared at her for a while. Finally I asked, "I know what your therapist has said, but how do *you* really feel?" I have never forgotten her response. She paused for a moment. Then her lips began to tremble, her eyes began to moisten. She hung her head in her hands and said, "Oh God, I feel so guilty. I feel so terribly, terribly dirty."

There are no inconsequential sins. And there are no exceptions to the rule.

Grace Is Sufficient

Reality check: *Grace is sufficient when repentance is forthcoming.* Let me repeat, there are no inconsequential sins. You are not the exception to the rule . . . but grace is sufficient when repentance is forthcoming.

As you read the story of Achan, you might wonder if grace is anywhere to be found. The end of Achan was harsh and drastic. He and his entire family were stoned to death. Their bodies were burned and covered with rocks. In fact, everything he owned was burned and buried as well. Where was grace?

Wasn't grace available in the Old Testament? Yes, of course there was grace in the Old Testament. So what was the problem? Repentance was not forthcoming.

Retrace the story. God revealed that there was sin in the camp, and Joshua was charged with rooting it out. Everyone, including Achan, knew that Joshua was seeking the guilty party. At that moment, Achan could have stepped forward and said, "It is me, it is me . . . please forgive me." But he didn't. From the very beginning, he could have come clean, and the outcome, I personally believe, would have been much different. But he did not. Achan had his opportunity, but he missed it. He did not confess *until he was caught.*

Grace is sufficient when repentance is forthcoming. In Achan's case, repentance was not forthcoming. There will come a day when every person will repent, a day when every knee shall bow, and every tongue shall confess that Jesus Christ is Lord (see Philippians 2:9-11). But for many, it will be too late, because confession was not forthcoming.

We need never doubt the sufficiency of grace. If, at that moment, Achan had felt conviction, recognized his sin and said, "It is me . . . it is me . . . it is me," the outcome might have been different. Psalm 32:3-5 says it well:

> When I kept silent, my bones grew old through my groaning all the day long. For day and night Your hand was heavy upon me. . . . I acknowledged my sin to You, and my iniquity I have not hidden. I said, "I will confess my transgressions to the Lord," and You forgave the iniquity of my sin.

Our God is the God of the clean slate, who takes every sin and places it as far away as "the east is from the west" (103:12). He buries your iniquities in the depth of the sea and remembers them no more (see Micah 7:19; Jeremiah 31:34). He takes sins that are as scarlet and makes them as white as snow (Isaiah 1:18). "If [we] will confess our sins, He is faithful and just to forgive us our sins and to cleanse us from all unrighteousness" (1 John 1:9). Grace is sufficient to forgive you and give you a second chance and, if need be, a brand-new life. If the life you have lived is too far gone to restore, He will start all over with you and build a new one.

The story is told of a man who had a warehouse to sell. It had been empty for years and had not been kept up. Finally, a buyer expressed interest in the property. The owner met the prospective buyer at the warehouse. When he saw the condition of his property, he was embarrassed. The doors were off their hinges and the glass was broken out of the windows. The entire place was full of trash, with rats running everywhere. Afraid he might lose the sell, the owner assured the potential buyer, "If you buy this property, I promise to put the doors back on the hinges, fix the windows, clean up the trash and get rid of the rats."

"Don't bother," the buyer replied, "I don't want the building. I just want the lot that it sits on. I'm going to build something brand-new on it."

When I think about it, that is precisely what God does. We worry so much about fixing our lives because they're such a mess, but God says, "I don't want your life. I want your heart. I plan to build a new life on it." Grace is always sufficient.

Discussion Questions

1. "There are no inconsequential sins." Do you agree with this statement and, if so, to what degree?

2. If our sins are forgiven, are they still consequential?

3. Have you known someone who seemed to be the exception to the rule? How can you explain this?

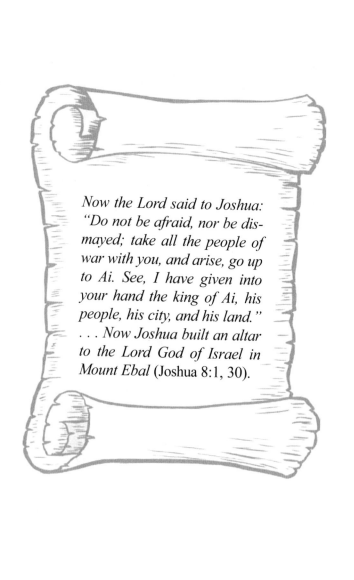

Now the Lord said to Joshua: "Do not be afraid, nor be dismayed; take all the people of war with you, and arise, go up to Ai. See, I have given into your hand the king of Ai, his people, his city, and his land." . . . Now Joshua built an altar to the Lord God of Israel in Mount Ebal (Joshua 8:1, 30).

10

The God of Second Chances

I wish I could tell you that the promised life is a life of constant success and no failures . . . that it will be a life of uninterrupted forward momentum . . . that perfection is within your reach. I wish I could tell you all of these things, but I cannot.

By now in our study, this should be clear. The bad news is, like Joshua and the children of Israel, you will blow it from time to time. You will disappoint God and yourself, and wonder how you managed to get into such a mess. Believe me, I know this from experience. But failure need not be final. You know the drill: If at first you don't succeed—try, try again. Failures are not people who fall down. Failures are people who fall down and don't get up. The good news is, our God has always been, and will always be, the God of second chances, and for that matter, third chances, and fourth and fifth, and so on.

Joshua 8 records two events. In the first half of the chapter, we are told of the destruction of Ai. Then, beginning with verse 30, we have an odd story of Joshua and the children of Israel at a place called Shechem

(Sychar)—camped between two mountains, reading the laws of God, and recommitting themselves to His laws. As you read the stories, they seem disconnected, but they are not.

What do these stories have in common? Through both events, God is giving Israel a second chance. Together they confirm this never-changing reality: Our God is the God of second chances. The children of Israel had made a mess of things. Having defeated mighty Jericho, they moved on to do battle with tiny Ai.

Again, it is important that we remember the geopolitical significance of Jericho and Ai. Jericho guarded the mountain passes that led up to the central highlands, and Ai sat just beyond it. Ai was the next obstacle to overcome. However, there was a problem. Sin had gotten into the camp, and because of sin, tiny Ai was able to defeat them.

Chapter 7 tells the story of Joshua cleansing the camp of its sin. Then we come to chapter 8, and it is as though God says, "Now that you've gotten it right, now that you've set things straight—go back to Ai." This time, with God's blessing, they totally annihilate the city. Joshua then goes up to Mount Ebal and calls all the people together for a time of recommitment to the laws of God.

I don't want to make this say more than it does. It would be very easy to take this passage of Scripture and stretch it. But what it does say is this: God is the God of second chances.

That is good news. It certainly is for me. I am a "second chancer." I have come to the Lord so often for second chances. Perhaps you have had the experience of frequenting a restaurant so often that the waiters and waitresses know what you normally order. As soon as you sit down, they ask, "The usual?" At times, I feel that way with God.

I fall on my knees and say, "Father, it's me again." And I can almost hear Him ask, "The usual?"

Second Chancers

I am not alone. As you read through the Scripture, you will be impressed with the number of second-chance people you find. The Bible is replete with second chancers—people of God who have blown it. Consider this partial list of examples.

1. *Abraham was a second chancer.* God had promised him and his wife, Sarah, that they would have a child. But as time went on and nothing happened, they lost faith in the promise. They didn't trust God to keep His word. Instead, they took matters into their own hands and blew it. When Sarah did not conceive, Abraham had an illicit relationship with Sarah's handmaiden, Hagar, and from that illegitimate relationship, a child was born. But he was not the child of promise. You would think in the face of such blatant unbelief God would have thrown up His hands in disgust and given up on them, but He did not. God gave them a second chance. The name of that second chance was Isaac.

2. *Jacob was a second chancer.* Jacob was a man with a destiny, but he drifted from God. At a place called Bethel, Jacob saw a vision of God's angels ascending and descending. Years later, he came back to Bethel, and God gave him another chance.

3. *Moses was a second chancer.* Groomed by life to be mightily used of God, Moses was a true believer living in the court of Pharaoh. It was no accident that a Hebrew was privileged to grow up as a prince of Egypt. The Lord had big plans for Moses, but Moses blew it. He killed an

Egyptian and was forced to flee for his life to the back-side of the wilderness of Midian. It took 40 years for him to get things right. But God gave Moses a second chance in the form of a burning bush, and the rest is history.

4. *Samson was a second chancer.* Samson was the heavyweight champion of the Old Testament, a mighty man who was able to tear a lion in half with his bare hands. He killed 1,000 Philistines with the jawbone of a donkey. Unfortunately, Samson had a weakness for women. You know the story. First, he lost his heart to a woman, then he lost his hair to her. Samson blew it and was reduced to slavery and animal servitude. But God didn't give up on him. God gave him a second chance. God used him mightily. In the end, Samson's greatest claim to fame was not that he was a mighty man, but rather that he was a second chancer.

5. *Jonah was a second chancer.* In fact, Jonah is the most noted second chancer in the entire Bible. Every preacher who has ever struggled with his calling knows his story by heart. Jonah was called to preach to the Ninevites. To say that Jonah didn't like Ninevites would be an under-statement. He did not want to preach to them, because he feared that they would hear and repent. God would then spare them, and Jonah didn't want them to be spared.

Jonah faced a dilemma. His solution? He got in a boat and headed in the opposite direction, toward Tarshish. However, God had other plans. He was not about to give up on Jonah or the Ninevites that easily. A storm arose. Jonah's shipmates realized he was the reason and tossed him overboard, and a great fish immediately swallowed him. End of story? Not quite. In fact, things are just get-ting started. For three days and nights, Jonah wallows in the gastric juices of that whale, until finally, he repented.

I don't know about you, but I doubt it would have taken me three days and three nights to repent. The moment that fish opened his mouth, and I saw that slimy gullet coming my way, I would have repented. I suspect every known sin would be confessed before I hit bottom. Jonah, however, was stubborn; he was recalcitrant. It took three days and three nights before he finally got it. He was thrown up on dry ground. Then we read one of the most remarkable statements in the Bible: "The word of the Lord came to Jonah the second time" (3:1). Jonah is a second chancer.

6. *David was a second chancer.* David, a man after God's own heart, committed adultery with Bathsheba, murdered Uriah, and then lied to cover it all up. But God didn't give up on David. He gave him another chance.

We could continue into the New Testament. Almost everyone who followed Christ was a second-chance person, including Paul, Philip, Thomas and Peter. Peter even cursed and denied that he knew Jesus. He told a servant girl that he had never even met the Man. But the Lord didn't give up on Peter.

Most of us would never have given Peter a second chance. We would have called him a coward, a scoundrel, a hypocrite. But the Lord knew something about Peter. He knew that Peter was just a human being with feet of clay. Incidentally, do not be surprised, or get discouraged, when Christians falter and fail. Don't assume that they are insincere. People are just people. We all have feet of clay. It is people like Peter and you and me that the Lord gives second chances. Aren't you glad?

I have already admitted that I am a second chancer. How about you? I suspect that there are a number of second chancers who will read this book. In fact, most who will be drawn to a book like this are second-chance people. There is no shortage of people who have messed up and in many different ways. Some of us have made a mess of our relationships. Our marriages are falling apart. In fact, many have ended in divorce. If you are one who has been through that terrible pain, can I give you a bit of good news? Divorce is not the unforgivable sin. God is the God of second chances.

Some of us have made unwise decisions; we've blown it. Some of those decisions have involved moral failure. If you have blown it, you can become one of God's second-chance people. One of my favorite verses in the entire Bible is found in one of the most difficult books to study, Lamentations. Speaking of God's mercy, it simply says, "They are [made] new every morning" (3:23). Every morning is a second chance, another opportunity.

Second Chances

All of this sounds so good. It is as good as it sounds, but it's not as simple as you might think. There are a few things we need to understand. If you have blown it, there is a second chance for you, but don't think it will be easy.

1. *Second chances are not easy outs.* Some might misunderstand, thinking, *So what if I fail? I get another chance.* Second chances are not easy solutions. They can come at a high price. David got a second chance, but read the rest of the story. You will discover that he paid a high price for that second chance.

It was the same for Abraham. He got a second chance, but at a high cost. The world has been paying for Abraham's second chance ever since. Joshua and the children of Israel got a second chance, but it was no easy out. In fact, as you read chapter 8, you discover it was harder to defeat little Ai than it was mighty Jericho. Second chances are not easy outs. When you blow it, you pay a price. Don't think for a moment that missing God's will is no big deal. It is a very big deal. When you fail morally, when your relationships end, there is a high price to pay. Be careful not to presume upon the grace of God. God does give second chances, but they're not easy outs.

2. *Second chances are not always like first chances.* Sometimes when you blow it, you can't go back again. There are times when life must move in new directions. Your second chance may require that you give up your first dreams. Perhaps God gave you a thriving ministry, but you had a moral failure. Sin has robbed you of your witness. God may give you a second chance, but you may never be able to minister where and how you once did. Perhaps you failed in your marriage. God may give you a second chance at happiness, but it might not involve marriage. For some, the second chance will require a new start and a different life.

3. *Second chances come in God's time and at His discretion.* Joshua was given a second chance almost immediately. But I have to tell you it does not always happen this way. It took Moses 40 years to receive his second chance.

David went through months—perhaps even years—of spiritual dryness and guilt before God restored the joy of his salvation. Jonah had to experience the gullet of a whale for three days and nights before he was ready for his second chance. Samson endured imprisonment and humiliation before his strength was restored, and ultimately, it cost his life.

I have known many that were made to wait. Some were old and at the end of life before God restored them.

I have been delighted to read in the last few years of God's restoration of televangelist Jim Bakker. I cannot recall of anyone in recent history who had a more public fall from grace. It is hard to believe that so many years have passed. From all I have read, I have concluded that Jim Bakker was a good man caught up in a bad deal. He made some serious mistakes. He committed some serious sins. But I believe he was far less guilty and far more repentant than some other well-known Christian celebrities have been. Yet, he went through so much heartache: imprisoned, humiliated, alone and abandoned. His marriage ended, and his life was ruined. It seemed that the God of the second chance had made an exception for him. But now, by all accounts, God is restoring him. And I, for one, am glad.

But why not sooner? I do not know. All I know is second chances are at God's discretion and in His time. Don't give up. "They that wait upon the Lord shall renew their strength; they shall mount up with wings as eagles" (Isaiah 40:31). Your day will come! Just wait upon the Lord. Have you fallen? Get up! Have you failed? It need not be final! Try, try again.

"So I will restore to you the years that the swarming locust has eaten. . . . You shall eat in plenty and be satisfied, and praise the name of the Lord your God, who has dealt wondrously with you" (Joel 2:25, 26).

Discussion Questions

1. To what extent do you consider yourself to be a "second chancer"?

2. How many second chances will God give?

3. Is your church a place of second chances?

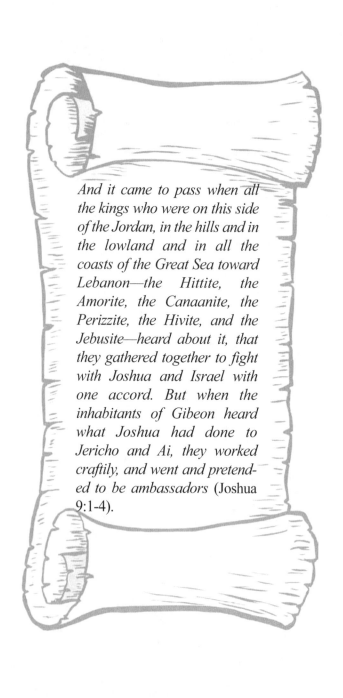

And it came to pass when all the kings who were on this side of the Jordan, in the hills and in the lowland and in all the coasts of the Great Sea toward Lebanon—the Hittite, the Amorite, the Canaanite, the Perizzite, the Hivite, and the Jebusite—heard about it, that they gathered together to fight with Joshua and Israel with one accord. But when the inhabitants of Gibeon heard what Joshua had done to Jericho and Ai, they worked craftily, and went and pretended to be ambassadors (Joshua 9:1-4).

11

Don't Be Stupid

I have a T-shirt at home that I never wear. It was a gift from my daughter, so I would like to put it on occasionally, but I fear it might cause a negative reaction. On the front of the shirt are printed these words: "People are stupid." On the back it reads: "You are a people."

I realize that some people find the word *stupid* to be offensive. Frankly, I don't understand this. Granted, my T-shirt is a bit insulting. But as far as I am concerned, *stupid* is a perfectly good word. I don't mean to be crude, but let me be blunt. There are some things in life that can be described with no other word. And the truth is, all of us are prone to those things. To quote Forrest Gump, "Stupid is as stupid does." I couldn't agree more. And all of us from time to time "do stupid."

I have good news, and I have bad news concerning this problem. First the bad news: God will not necessarily keep you from the consequences of your own stupidity. Ouch! Now the good news: God will not abandon you just because you make a foolish choice.

If you learn those two truths, you will be head and

137

shoulders above most people. We tend to get this backward. We think if God really loves us, He will keep us from the consequences of our choices. When God does not keep us from the consequences, we assume He has abandoned us because of our foolish decision. This isn't true. Let me repeat: God will not keep you from the consequences of your stupidity, but He will not abandon you when you do something stupid. Praise God for that! If He did, none of us would be able to live the promised life.

Joshua learned these two truths the hard way. In chapters 9 and 10, he suffers the consequences of a dumb choice. To make matters worse, it was his foolishness that caused the problem. The story is complex. Joshua and the children of Israel were fully engaged in the conquest of the land. Scholars refer to this part of the conquest as the Southern Campaign. Word has quickly spread throughout the entire land that the Israelites were a force with which to be reckoned. Everyone was looking for a way to survive their advance. Warring factions soon came together in various alliances, ready to defend themselves.

But one group had another plan. The Gibeonites sent representatives to seek peace. They came with a convincing argument. Paraphrased, it went something like this:

> We have come not as your enemies; we have come as your friends. We are not bad, we are good. We do not mean to do you ill, we mean to do you well. We are not even from here. We have come from a far country. We even believe in the same God you believe in. We have but one desire, that you make a covenant of peace with us. This covenant will be good for you, and it will be good for us. Good for us because we will not be

attacked. Good for you because it will extend your influence over more people and your rule over more land (see 9:6-13).

All of this sounded good. However, there was one problem: it was all a lie. They were not friends—they were enemies. They were not from a far country—they were from Canaan. In fact, their home was just three days' journey away. They did not mean to do well by the Israelites; they meant to do them ill. And they were not believers; they were pagans. All this was a ruse. But in haste—under pressure and without prayer—Joshua entered into a covenant with them. "Stupid is as stupid does."

The Bad News

Unfortunately, Joshua now faced the first law of stupid behavior. God will not necessarily keep us from the consequences of our own stupidity. Even after he discovered he had been duped and the wool had been pulled over his eyes, God would not release him from the covenant. He allowed Joshua to suffer the consequences of his foolish choice. From that moment forward, he would have the Gibeonites on his hands.

Joshua was angry when he discovered their deceit and vowed that they would not enjoy their new peace. They would become servants for as long as they existed as a people. But the covenant would continue.

And that day Joshua made them woodcutters and water carriers for the congregation and for the altar of the Lord, in the place which He would choose, even to this day (v. 27).

139

Note the key phrase, *even to this day*. Keep in mind that this account was written many years later. If Joshua was the writer, he is by now an old man. Looking back, he remembers the time when he made a foolish decision to enter into a covenant with the Gibeonites. Now many years later, they are still water carriers and woodcutters in the house of the Lord. In other words, many years have passed, and the Gibeonites are still under foot. But it did not end there. The consequences of this decision continued for many generations.

Let's fast-forward 400 years. In 2 Samuel, God is angry with Saul. Why? Because Saul desires to break the covenant with the Gibeonites. Four hundred years after Joshua's foolish choice, the Gibeonites are still under foot.

Fast-forward again 900 years to the time of Ezra. Ezra is trying to rebuild Jerusalem, but he is having trouble. He runs into problems with . . . guess who? The Gibeonites. Nine hundred years after the fact, one foolish decision is plaguing the people.

This is a hard lesson to learn, but learn it well. God will not necessarily keep you from the consequences of your own stupidity. I believe God puts a hedge of protection around His people, but we can step outside the hedge when we make foolish choices.

- Two young lovers under pressure—in haste, certainly without prayer—make a foolish decision. She becomes pregnant; the consequences will be lived out for the rest of their lives.

- In anger, a husband and wife make a decision to end a marriage. They will live with the consequence of that decision for years to come, and so will their children.

- A businessman has an opportunity to make a profit, though he knows that the deal is shaky at best, and shady at worst. The deal falls through. A foolish choice has been made, and the result is that a reputation and a business is destroyed. Now he must live with the consequences.

Joshua made a foolish decision, and God did not clean up the mess. This was a hard lesson, but he learned it well. Joshua never made this mistake again.

Keeping Your Head

How do we avoid doing foolish things? I don't think we can entirely, certainly not easily. Stupidity is like sin. We will always struggle with it to one degree or another. And sooner or later, we will make a mistake; we will do "dumb" things. But there are some things we can do to lessen our vulnerability. We can learn to be wise. How does this happen? There are no simple formulas, but there are some safeguards we can put in place.

1. *The fear of the Lord.* The Bible says this is the "beginning of wisdom" (Psalm 111:10; Proverbs 9:10). A loose paraphrase might be: "Wisdom begins when walking in His will becomes your first priority." When your first fear is missing God, you become much wiser. I have discovered when I fear stepping outside the will of God, I am far less likely to do so.

2. *The Word of God.* "But you must continue in the things which you have learned and been assured of, knowing from whom you have learned them, and that from childhood you have known the Holy Scriptures, which are able to make you wise" (2 Timothy 3:14, 15). There is a wisdom that can come no other way. "All

Scripture is given by inspiration of God, and is profitable for doctrine, for reproof, for correction, for instruction in righteousness" (v. 16).

Who is wiser, the man who has read all other books except the Bible, or the man who has read no other books except the Bible? If you always seem to make the wrong decision, check the Scripture quotient in your life.

3. *Common sense.* There is nothing unspiritual about simply using your head. Ninety percent of living the promised life is learning to do so. In fact, 90 percent of walking by faith is just using your head. Jesus said, "Behold, I send you out as sheep in the midst of wolves. Therefore, be wise as serpents and harmless as doves" (Matthew 10:16). We are more likely to be as harmless as doves than to be as wise as serpents. In Luke 16, Jesus makes a remarkable statement: "The sons of this world are more shrewd in their generation than the sons of light" (v. 8). To paraphrase, sometimes the devil's crowd uses their head more than God's people do. Too many Christians seem to believe that thinking negates faith. Nonsense! Use your head. Common sense is the ability to think of the consequence before you act.

4. *Spiritual discernment.* There will be times when the fear of God, the knowledge of Scripture and common sense will not be enough. Without spiritual discernment, you will be fooled. It is important to remember that things are not always what they seem. Not everything that looks good, is good. In fact, I have never known evil to appear as evil. Evil always disguises itself as good. Evil doesn't just jump out at you and say, "Ha! I'm going to destroy you!" Evil camouflages itself either by looking benign or good. Joshua was not drawn into something that looked bad—he was drawn into something that looked good.

A young woman wants to be a godly woman. Her desire is to be what God wants her to be, but then she meets a young man. He does not look bad, he looks good. He says all the right things. The problem is he is not a Christian, or if he is, he is nominally so. She loves him, and she loves the Lord. Over time, however, that which looks good begins to draw her away from her spiritual roots. She ignores the fact that they are unequally yoked. She finds herself being less spiritually committed and more involved with this young man. Something that looked good has drawn her away from God's purpose in her life. Incidentally, any relationship that makes you less spiritual is evil disguised as good.

A young man desires to be a godly man. He wants to be the kind of father and husband God wants him to be. A career opportunity comes his way. It seems like a good deal. The only problem is, it will require his constant attention. He will have little time for his wife and kids. However, he rationalizes by thinking it will provide a great lifestyle for his family. There would be plenty of money for not only the things they need, but all the things they want as well. He spends less and less time with his family, and has less and less time for his faith. What looked good wasn't good at all.

Without discernment, we will be in trouble. Learn to listen to that still small voice within. My experience is that if I will listen, the Spirit will direct. Learn to follow the peace of your heart more than the passion of your head. Often when you have a decision to make, you will sense a peace about it or a lack thereof. Learn to trust this inner voice. More often than not, it is the voice of the Spirit.

The Good News

God will not abandon you just because you make a foolish choice. If you follow the story through chapter 10, you discover something amazing. God takes the children of Israel, Gibeonites and all, and moves forward with them. Joshua 10 is a remarkable account of an unprecedented miracle—God causes time to stand still in order for Joshua to win a major battle. But the truly remarkable thing about the entire chapter is that it follows chapter 9. Joshua had made a foolish choice, but God picked him up right where he was and moved on. Rather than abandon us when we make stupid mistakes, God picks us up right where we are—right where our choices have left us—and moves us forward.

No doubt someone will ask, "If God has not abandoned me, where is He in all of this?" He is right in the middle of the circumstance that your foolish choice has created.

Where is God in the life of the teenage girl who got pregnant out of wedlock and now has a child? He is right there with her helping her raise that child. Where is God in the life of the woman whose foolish choice left her a single mother? He is right there with her, helping her, giving her the strength to carry on.

Are you a man who has destroyed your reputation by a poor moral choice? Do you wonder where God is in your life? He is right there with you, helping you rebuild your reputation from the ground up.

Our choices create circumstances, and God is right there in them with us. He takes us right where our choices leave us, and He moves forward with our lives— Gibeonites and all. That sounds like another "grace thing" to me.

Discussion Questions

1. What is the difference in a mistake and a sin? Can a mistake be a sin?

2. Does a foolish choice always place us outside of God's protective hedge?

3. How do you discern the "still small voice" of God?

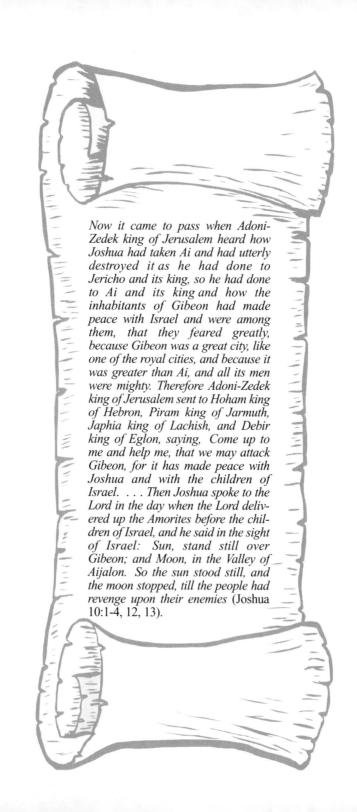

Now it came to pass when Adoni-Zedek king of Jerusalem heard how Joshua had taken Ai and had utterly destroyed it as he had done to Jericho and its king, so he had done to Ai and its king and how the inhabitants of Gibeon had made peace with Israel and were among them, that they feared greatly, because Gibeon was a great city, like one of the royal cities, and because it was greater than Ai, and all its men were mighty. Therefore Adoni-Zedek king of Jerusalem sent to Hoham king of Hebron, Piram king of Jarmuth, Japhia king of Lachish, and Debir king of Eglon, saying, Come up to me and help me, that we may attack Gibeon, for it has made peace with Joshua and with the children of Israel. . . . Then Joshua spoke to the Lord in the day when the Lord delivered up the Amorites before the children of Israel, and he said in the sight of Israel: Sun, stand still over Gibeon; and Moon, in the Valley of Aijalon. So the sun stood still, and the moon stopped, till the people had revenge upon their enemies (Joshua 10:1-4, 12, 13).

12

The Promise of Providence

If you can keep your head while everyone around you is losing theirs, it may be a sign that you don't appreciate how bad things are. You may not fully understand the problem. This could be true. However, there is another possibility. If you can keep your head while everyone around you is losing theirs, it could be a sign that you appreciate how good God is. You may understand providence.

Let me define *providence*. *Providence* is that remarkable capacity of God to take every circumstance of my life and "work all things together" (see Romans 8:28). Please note that I said, "Work all things together," not "Work all things out." There is a difference between these two. From time to time, I hear people express their confidence that God will work all things out. By that, they mean that somehow in the end everything will work out to their satisfaction. Not so. God does not promise to work all things out to our liking. He does promise to work out all things together to our good. While the clearest statement of this is found in Romans, one of the most fascinating examples is found in Joshua 10.

147

This is an incredible passage of Scripture. It is the story of Joshua's long day. Let me set the scene. In chapter 9, Joshua made a treaty with the Gibeonites. It was a foolish treaty, promising the Gibeonites that they would not only be spared attack from Israel, but they would also come under their protection if attacked by anyone else. From the outset, Joshua was forced to live up to this agreement. In chapter 10, we are told of five Amorite kings who find out about the treaty. Jealous and angry, they assemble against Gibeon. Having made a treaty with them, Joshua must now protect the Gibeonites.

Joshua force-marched his army to the Valley of Aijalon to do battle with these five kings. When Joshua arrived, he realized that he faced a rare moment of opportunity. In the valley before him were all five major kings of that region. This was an unprecedented target of opportunity. If he destroys these five kings, he will not only win this battle, but the entire campaign for the south will also be won. If he can defeat these kings here, he will not have to spend months, perhaps even years, fighting them on their home ground. The battle was on.

At first, things went splendidly. From the onset, the battle was clearly turned in their favor. However, there was one insurmountable problem—they were running out of time. The sun was setting. Joshua feared that the enemy would escape under the cover of darkness. So he turned to the Lord and cried, "Sun, stand still over Gibeon; and Moon, in the Valley of Aijalon." At that point, the Scripture says a most remarkable thing. The sun stood still, and the moon did not move. God extended the time by a period of a whole day.

The Miracle

This is one of the most mind-boggling and faith-challenging miracles in the entire Bible. It is, incidentally, not the only miracle in this passage. There is a lot more happening in this passage than the sun and moon standing still. As you read this account, you will discover that there are other things taking place that some might not consider miraculous, but clearly they were. In verse 11 we read:

> And it happened, as they fled before Israel and were on the descent of Beth Horon, that the Lord cast down large hailstones from heaven on them as far as Azekah, and they died. There were more who died from the hailstones than the children of Israel killed with the sword.

This was a hailstorm. Hailstorms happen in almost every part of the world. In our own country, we have hailstorms so violent that hail the size of softballs and larger can fall, potentially penetrating the roof of a house and killing a person. You might read this and think that the hailstorm was not a miracle, but rather a strange coincidence. Give God some credit. Things that don't look like miracles have God's hand involved in them.

I love the old story of the man who took his wife deer hunting. When he explained how everything worked, she replied, "There is nothing to this—any idiot can do it." So he set her up in a tree stand, and he went 200 yards away to another stand. He was there only about half an hour, when he heared four shots ring out—POW, POW, POW, POW! Climbing down out of the tree, he ran to his wife's location. When he arrived, he saw that she was still up in the tree, with her gun pointed down at a man whose arms were raised in the air as he said, "OK, lady, whatever you say; it's a deer, it's a deer. Just let me get my saddle off first." I don't care what you call a miracle; a miracle is a miracle.

The hailstorm was miraculous, but the focal point of this passage is the miracle of time standing still. I would love to have this miracle repeated at times in my own life. Who wouldn't love to be able to extend time? I don't know a mother anywhere who wouldn't like to add a few hours to her day. I love this miracle, but I have to be honest and tell you that no miracle in the Bible gives me more trouble. I don't have trouble believing other miracles, but I have difficulty with this one, though there is good evidence to support it.

It stands to reason if there was a long day for Joshua and the children of Israel, there had to have been a long day for other people as well. Throughout history, there have been other long days recorded. The ancient Babylonians have in their records an account of an incredibly long day, as do the ancient Assyrians, the ancient Chinese, the Aztecs and the Incas. But in spite of all the historic confirmation, I still have a hard time with this miracle.

Frankly, I don't have a hard time believing Peter walked upon the water, or that Jesus turned water into wine. I don't even have a hard time believing 5,000 people can be fed with just five loaves and two fish, but this miracle throws me for a loop. I find it difficult to believe that the sun could stand still and the moon not move. But I want you to know, I do believe it.

Some of you just sighed a sigh of relief. I had you on the edge of your seat. I do believe it, but I have to tell you that I believe it purely by faith. I believe it because I choose to believe that the Scripture is the accurate record of what God has done. R.G. Lee felt the same way when he said, "If a man can make a clock, he can stop it." Well, I think if God creates time, God can extend it. I don't know how God did this—but by faith, I believe He did.

The Message

The centerpiece of this passage is clearly this great miracle. We can't help but be impressed with it. However, I fear we might be so enamored with this miracle that we miss the message in it. This story is not recorded just so we will be impressed with the omnipotence of God. There is a far greater message in this passage. It's about providence. It's about God moving heaven and earth or, in this case, halting heaven and earth, in order to work all things together to good for His people.

Remember what is happening. You have the five Caananite kings gathered in one place. Talk about a target of opportunity. How did this happen? Was it just dumb luck? As I read this, I see God working all things together. In the previous story, Joshua made a foolish decision to enter into an alliance with the Gibeonites. It was a dumb thing to do. That decision would bear consequences for generations to come. But in chapter 10, God uses that bad choice as the instrument to bring all those kings together in one place. Joshua's dumb decision was being used by God to His ends. In other words, God was working all things together.

Now I don't know what that says to you, but to me it says that our God is the God of providence. The Bible says that all things work together for good to those who love the Lord. That's a promise; you can take it to the bank.

There is an important point here we need to understand.

Most people think that the promise of providence guarantees that when bad things happen, they will ultimately work to our good. But there is more to it than that. The Bible is not just referring to the tragedies that come *to* us; I also believe God works in the stupidities that come *from* us. This is the point of this passage. God has this wonderful way of using our mistakes—even sins—to our good. Don't misinterpret that. We have already seen that sin is serious and mistakes carry a consequence. But the hope of providence is that God can overcome our foolishness. I can't tell you how comforting that is to know.

This is what makes me an optimist, not a pessimist. I watch the pessimistic, hopeless demeanor of so many Christians and wonder, *Where does this hopelessness come from?*

Someone made the distinction between an optimist and a pessimist. Two optimists meet and shake hands; two pessimists meet and shake heads. That is exactly where so many people are. But why? Maybe the problem lies in the fact that we lack confidence in Providence.

I am not worried about all that is happening on the world's stage. I do not know if it will all work out, but I do know it will all work together. I do not know if all the circumstances of my life will work out, but I do know they will all work together. God has promised that all things will work together for the good of those who love God, and I love Him. That is where my hope rests.

The way I figure it, if God can stop the sun in its tracks, He can take care of my little life. He *can* and *will* work all things together, even if He has to move heaven and earth to do it. That's what I believe. What do you believe?

Discussion Questions

1. What is the difference between the statements "Everything will work out" and "All things will work together?"

2. Can sinful behavior work together for good? If so, how?

3. Can you see evidence of God's providence in your life?

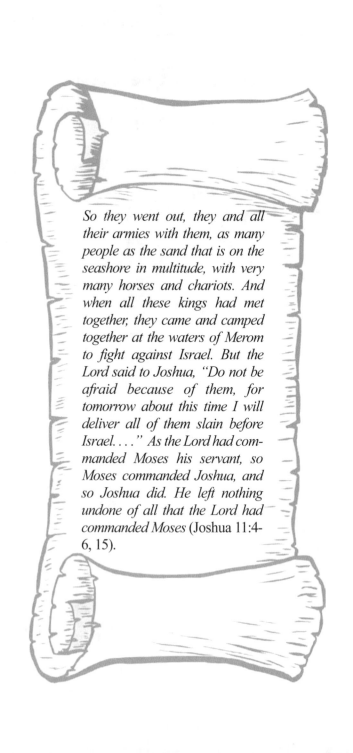

So they went out, they and all their armies with them, as many people as the sand that is on the seashore in multitude, with very many horses and chariots. And when all these kings had met together; they came and camped together at the waters of Merom to fight against Israel. But the Lord said to Joshua, "Do not be afraid because of them, for tomorrow about this time I will deliver all of them slain before Israel. . . ." As the Lord had commanded Moses his servant, so Moses commanded Joshua, and so Joshua did. He left nothing undone of all that the Lord had commanded Moses (Joshua 11:4-6, 15).

13

Learning How to Win

In a now infamous 1990 speech, television mogul Ted Turner referred to Christianity as a "religion for losers." The firestorm that followed his statement has yet to die down. More than 13 years later, he is still being criticized for his remarks. By his own admission, he has come to regret the comment.

Frankly, I don't understand what all the fuss is about. Ted Turner is right. Christianity is a religion for losers. The only problem with Ted's thinking is that he doesn't seem to understand that without Christ, we are all losers. Did you know that God loves losers? It is a good thing He does; otherwise, there would be no church. The fact that God loves losers is good news. But there is even better news—God builds winners. He loves losers, but He doesn't want losers to remain that way. He wants losers to become winners.

By definition, the church is a bunch of losers striving to become winners. The question is, How does this happen? How do whiners become winners? How do chumps become champs? Can losers learn how to win? Indeed they can.

The Book of Joshua could easily be titled "Learning How to Win." The story begins with a bunch of losers wandering aimlessly around in a desert. But as the story progresses, these losers learn how to win. No place in the book is this more evident than in chapters 11–14. These chapters comprise the account of Joshua's northern campaign. Chapter 10 concluded the campaign for the southern part of Canaan. Beginning with chapter 11, Joshua and the children of Israel move north to conquer the rest of the land. By this time, they have learned how to win. The list of victories is astonishing. Never had a people been so successful in possessing a land. God's people, who were once losers, have now clearly become winners.

Winning was something the children of Israel had to learn. It did not come naturally for them . . . it doesn't come naturally for most of us. If you want to be a winner, you will, in all likelihood, have to learn how. There may be a few folks who are naturally victorious, but most of us are, at best, winners in training.

Bobby Cox, the manager of the Atlanta Braves, was being interviewed after the Braves had won the World Series, having tried twice before. When asked, "What is the difference in this team and the other two?" he replied, "We have finally learned how to win."

The promised life is much like that. You must learn *how* to win. This is so important. I encounter so many defeated people—people who live under, not over, the problems of life. Rather than singing "Victory in Jesus," they could sing more honestly "Misery in Jesus." It does not have to be that way. How do losers become winners? Perhaps a better way of asking the question is, What do winners do that losers don't?

Winners Risk Failure

Do you always play it safe? Do you never go out on a limb? If so, you seldom ever win, *because winners take risks.* The bottom line is, if you are going to win with the Lord and live the promised life, you must put some things on the line. If you never get out of the boat and take a chance, you will never walk on water.

Let me remind you why the children of Israel had been in the wilderness in the first place. For 40 years they wandered in the wilderness for one reason: an older generation before them had not been willing to take a chance. When given the opportunity to claim the land in their day, they decided to play it safe.

For the next 40 years, the children of Israel did just that. They played it safe, until one day the Lord said to Joshua, "It is time to stop playing it safe. This bunch of chumps needs to become a bunch of champs. Cross over the river." To conquer the land, they had to risk failure. Once again, Joshua and the children of Israel faced a great challenge. If the conquest was to continue, they must risk failure again. This time, the risk was greater than ever. All the northern kings had gathered together in a place called Mizpah. "So they went out, they and all their armies with them, as many people as the sand that is on the seashore in multitude, with very many horses and chariots" (11:4).

Joshua faced an enemy unlike any he had ever faced. He has already overcome some formidable opposition by defeating Jericho and Ai, the Amorite kings in the Valley of Aijalon, and the entire southern half of the land. But he had never been up against an army that was so large and well-equipped.

Scripture describes the enemy as having horses and chariots. As far as we know, Joshua did not have horses and chariots. The Jewish historian Josephus described this army as having 300,000 foot soldiers, 30,000 horsemen, and 10,000 to 15,000 chariots. On paper, the children of Israel did not match up well. This was a "David versus Goliath" circumstance. It would have been easy for them to say, "This is too much . . . we had better play it safe." But they did not. By this time, Joshua understood this principle: Great victory requires great risk.

I don't know why we find this difficult to grasp. The rest of the world seems to have caught on. Businessmen know this. Business people who are good at what they do know that occasionally they have to take a chance. If you are not willing to risk failure, you will rarely know success. Your competition will leave you in the dust.

We know this in the realm of romance. You guys know if you never ask the girl out, there is no chance of a relationship with her. But if you ask her out, you risk rejection.

Farmers know this. Farmers know that if they don't put the seed in the ground, there will be no harvest. But there is always the risk that the crop will fail. We seem to know this in every walk of life, but we forget it when it comes to the faith.

Some Christians have the idea that they shouldn't take big risks. Ask average people in your community to name for you an organization that is truly cutting edge—out there and adventurous. You will talk a long, long time before anyone names the church. They will probably name some entrepreneur or developer. Perhaps they will mention someone involved with the latest experiments in medicine or education, but the church would not even be considered. We are not known as risk-taking people. We talk about the adventure of faith, but it is largely just that—talk. And if we do take a risk, it will all be minimal. What we really like to do is take little risks and claim big victories. We set little goals, accomplish them and have big celebrations when we do.

Imagine that you feel the need to prove your masculinity. To do so, you think it is necessary to get into a fistfight and beat someone up. I am your opponent of choice. So you proceed to beat me to a bloody pulp and leave me in a quivering mass on the floor. With victory well in hand, you dance around like Rocky in front of his statue in Philadelphia. Big deal. You beat up an out-of-shape, middle-aged preacher. Why don't you get in the ring with George Foreman, or Mike Tyson, or your wife? This is what we do in church. We take little risks and claim big victories.

Doesn't it seem odd that the least risk-taking people today are the very people who are supposedly living by faith? That is precisely why churches are so dull. I'm not advocating taking foolish risks. Use your head. But if you are going to win, you must risk failure.

May I remind you that God never played it safe with you? He sent forth His Son into the world. He left the realms of glory and took upon Himself the form of man. It doesn't sound like He was playing it safe. He risked rejection. Evidently, He believed you were worth the risk.

Winners Leave Nothing Undone

Winners follow through. In 11:1-15, Joshua describes just one battle. Beginning with verse 16, we are told of all the other battles that followed.

Thus Joshua took all this land: the mountain country, all the South, all the land of Goshen, the lowland, and the Jordan plain—the mountains of Israel and its lowlands, from Mount Halak and the ascent to Seir, even as far as Baal Gad in the Valley of Lebanon below Mount Hermon. He captured all their kings, and struck them down and killed them (vv. 16, 17).

After the main battle, there were many more. Verse 18 is a key verse. It says, "Joshua made war a long time with all those kings."

In chapter 12, beginning with verse 9, is a list of the 31 kings Joshua defeated. In other words, one battle led to the next battle, which led to the next battle, which led to the next battle, and Joshua didn't stop short.

But it does not end there. In 13:1, we read this: "Now Joshua was old, advanced in years. And the Lord said to him: 'You are old, advanced in years, and there remains very much land yet to be possessed.'"

Joshua spent seven years conquering the northern kingdom, and then he spent the rest of his life fighting clean-up battles, but he didn't stop short. In fact, let me show you an interesting verse that may be one of the most impressive in the entire story of Joshua.

As the Lord had commanded Moses his servant, so Moses commanded Joshua, and so Joshua did. He left nothing undone of all that the Lord had commanded Moses (11:15).

Notice the phrase "he left nothing undone." Winners do not play it safe, and they leave nothing undone. When I read this statement, it hit me like a bolt. *He left nothing undone.* What a testimony! Wouldn't you love to stand before the Lord and hear Him say, "Well done . . . you left nothing undone"?

What are you leaving undone in your life? Have you followed through with your dreams? Have you followed through with your relationships? Is there someone you need to forgive? A relationship you need to restore? What about your marriage? Is there something left undone between you and your mate? We leave so much undone in our moral lives. We have worked hard at being the person we ought to be, but there is that one area that is left undone.

What are you leaving undone in your faith? Perhaps in your relationship with God, there is something with which you have not followed through. Your decision to follow Christ is the beginning of faith, not the end. It is like marriage. You may think that when you say "I do," it's done. But it is not. It has only begun. The same thing happens in the faith. We make a profession of faith and think that's that. But that is just the beginning.

Our Lord did not play it safe; neither did He leave anything undone. He went all the way to the cross—all the way! In the Garden of Gethsemane, He could have backed away. He prayed, "Father . . . let this cup pass from Me" (Matthew 26:39). In other words, "I don't want to go through with this." But He went all the way to the cross, leaving nothing undone. As He hung on the cross, He said, "It is finished" (John 19:30), meaning nothing was left undone. What are you leaving undone in the faith?

Discussion Questions

1. Can we live by faith without taking risks?

2. If we take a risk and fail, does that necessarily mean that we took the wrong risk?

3. What are the things that you feel have been left undone in your life?

PART THREE

CLAIMING WHAT IS RIGHTFULLY YOURS

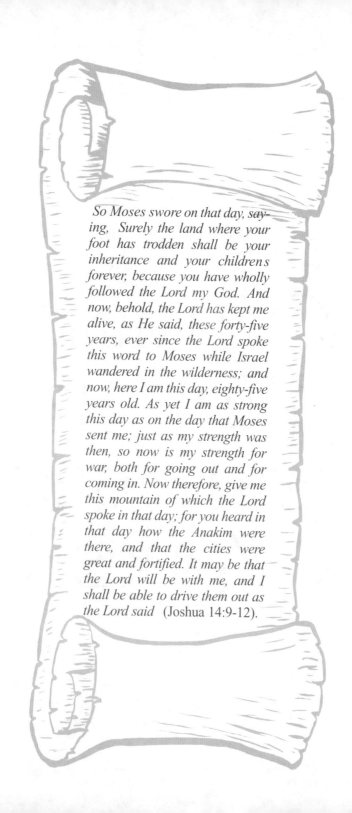

So Moses swore on that day, saying, Surely the land where your foot has trodden shall be your inheritance and your childrens forever, because you have wholly followed the Lord my God. And now, behold, the Lord has kept me alive, as He said, these forty-five years, ever since the Lord spoke this word to Moses while Israel wandered in the wilderness; and now, here I am this day, eighty-five years old. As yet I am as strong this day as on the day that Moses sent me; just as my strength was then, so now is my strength for war, both for going out and for coming in. Now therefore, give me this mountain of which the Lord spoke in that day; for you heard in that day how the Anakim were there, and that the cities were great and fortified. It may be that the Lord will be with me, and I shall be able to drive them out as the Lord said (Joshua 14:9-12).

14

A Profile in Character

This may sound a bit jaded, but I am not easily impressed. Maybe you are, but I have lived long enough to know that people are not always what they seem to be. But occasionally, I come across a truly impressive man or woman. I am not impressed with celebrity. I have never understood why anyone would be. I am not impressed with money. Why do we think someone who makes $200,000 a year is inherently better than someone who makes $20,000? I am not particularly impressed with appearance. Beauty fades quickly. What impresses me is character.

Joshua 14 is a rather obscure passage. It is the story of a man named Caleb. You may not be familiar with it. Caleb is seldom studied, but what a man Caleb was! He was the consummate man of character. Caleb was one of the original 12 spies sent out by Moses 45 years before. By this time, all the others are dead except for Joshua and him. Caleb was a man of integrity. God had given him a tremendous promise. Though more than 45 years had passed, he continued to believe God would keep His word.

Character is so important. There is, however, a difference between character and reputation.

Reputation . . .	Character . . .
What other people think of you	What God knows about you
Governs your behavior in the light	Governs your behavior in the dark
Causes a man to always be seen doing right things	Causes a man to always be doing the right thing even when he is not seen.

This is what is missing in our society today, yet it is necessary if we are to live the life of promise.

As we examine the life of Caleb, we will talk about attributes that produce character in the promised life.

Character Overcomes

Character always rises to the top. A person of character rises above circumstances, background and upbringing. A person of character does not play the victim.

Some background information is critical to our understanding of Caleb. He was born on "the wrong side of the tracks." Caleb was a man whose upbringing would not have guaranteed the position that he attained in life. Caleb was not an Israelite; he was a Kenizzite. "Hebron therefore became the inheritance of Caleb the son of Jephunneh the Kenizzite to this day, because he wholly followed the Lord God of Israel" (v. 14).

Bible scholars are divided on *what it means to be a Kenizzite.* The best suggestion is that the Kenizzites were people who lived in the land of Edom, who may be the same as the Edomites. But we do not know for certain who they were. We do know that they were not the children of Israel, and Caleb took his heritage from them. Caleb was a stranger in the land who became part of the people of God.

In 15:13, we read, "Now to Caleb the son of Jephunneh he gave a share among the children of Judah." He was not part of the children of Judah, but he was given the privilege of living among them. In 1 Chronicles, we find the genealogy of the people of God, and Caleb's family is left out all together. Why? Because Caleb's family were not Israelites; they were Kenizzites. He was an outsider.

Some of you know what it is like to be an outsider. Let me give you some good news.

God has an affinity for folks who are born without "a silver spoon in their mouth." The apostle Paul, speaking to the Christians in Corinth, implied that God chooses those no one else would choose.

> For you see your calling, brethren, that not many wise according to the flesh, not many mighty, not many noble, are called. But God has chosen the foolish things of the world to put to shame the wise, and God has chosen the weak things of the world to put to shame the things which are mighty; and the base things of the world and the things which are despised God has chosen, and the things which are not, to bring to nothing the things that are (1 Corinthians 1:26-28).

To paraphrase, God has chosen the disadvantaged. Some people would look down their noses at those God has chosen. God has said, "These are the very ones I will use." I have known many people who have done great things for God, and have struggled to overcome. It is character that causes them to rise above it all.

I deal with so many people who play the victim, who use their past as an excuse for their present behavior or circumstance. Character rises above circumstances . . . character overcomes.

Character Refuses to Settle

People with character do not give up their dreams. In this story, we have an 85-year-old man who will not settle for less than what God promised him. God told him that one day he would own a mountain called Hebron, and he would settle for nothing else.

Forty-five years earlier, Caleb and Joshua, along with 10 other spies, had entered Canaan. When they returned, 10 of the 12 said that the land was indeed flowing with milk and honey, but there were giants in the land (the sons of Anak, the Anakim); therefore, it could not be conquered.

The 10 spies said, "We were like grasshoppers . . . in their sight" (Numbers 13:33). These 10 were afraid, and they frightened all the rest. Caleb and Joshua, however, saw things differently.

They said, "With God, we can take this land" (see 14:7, 8). But the people listened to the majority report and refused to enter in. Moses, speaking for God, expressed his disappointment with the people and his pleasure with Joshua and Caleb (see vv. 19-24). Of those 12 spies, only they would enter the Promised Land. And for his faithfulness, Caleb would one day own a lush, verdant, beautiful mountain called Hebron. After 45 years had passed, he had still not given up on that promise.

Caleb did not allow age to rob him of his dream. I believe we have done a great disservice to senior adults. Through our culture, we have taught them that when they reach a certain age, they must stop striving for their dreams. Caleb was 85, an age when most say you should rest, not risk.

I am discovering something about the aging process; it is a matter of perspective. Have you noticed that when you are old, even the relatively old look young to you? If you are 80, someone who is 60 seems youthful. If you're 6 years old, a 16-year-old looks like an adult . . . and a 40-year-old seems ancient.

I love the story of the 6-year-old boy who asked his granddad, "Granddad, were you on the ark?" The grandfather replied, "No, Son, I wasn't on the ark." The little boy responded, "Well, why didn't you drown?"

It is all a matter of perspective. We tell people that when they reach a certain age, they must give up their dreams. Nonsense. If you are old, you have limited time to reach your goals.

I recently spoke at a National Senior Adult Conference. My message was well received by most, but not by all. I had only one main point: Don't stop living until you die. Evidently, some thought the message was a bit too straightforward. But the problem is very real. There are many people who stop living before they die. Not Caleb. At 85 years old, he still wanted his mountain.

John Wesley traveled over 250,000 miles in his lifetime—mostly by horseback. He preached over 40,000 sermons. At 80, he was preaching four times a day, until he was forced to slow down to only twice a day. Don't let age rob you of your dream.

Caleb did not allow other people to dissuade him.

Picture the scene: Caleb is talking to his family saying, "Forty-five years ago, I was promised a mountain, and I want what has been promised me." I can almost hear his family's response. His kids say: "Come on, Dad, you're 85. Give it up." His wife might have responded: "I've been listening to you talk about that mountain for 45 years. You are an old man. For heaven's sake, act your age."

Do not let other people dissuade you from your dream. Parents need to be careful not to discourage children from following the desire of their heart. Some of you were too afraid to follow your own dream, and now you are instilling that fear in your kids. Shame on you! Fear is contagious.

I was flying out of the McCarran International Airport in Las Vegas. I had been speaking in a little community called Overton, Nevada, just north of Las Vegas. It was my misfortune to be assigned to the middle seat between two rather large men. Being no Twiggy myself, I was wedged in. One of the men appeared to be a businessman; he wore a three-piece suit. The other man wore a beard and glasses. Though he could not smoke it, he was chewing on a pipe, and he was reading the travels of Marco Polo. I took him for an intellectual.

We started down the runway, and everything was going well until suddenly the pilot reversed the engines, veered off the runway, and came to a screeching halt. I have flown enough to know that sometimes plans do change suddenly. I was not terribly concerned, but the poor intellectual sitting next to me was terrified. He cried, "Oh, my God!" Then in a reflex reaction, he grabbed my knee. Initially, I was not afraid, but from that moment on, I found myself nervous and fearful. Fear is contagious. Other people's fear can dissuade us if we let it. Do not let other people dissuade you from your God-given dream. Character refuses to settle in life.

Character Stands Alone

"Nevertheless my brethren who went up with me made the heart of the people melt, but I wholly followed the Lord my God" (Joshua 14:8).

Caleb stood when no one else would. Except for Joshua, Caleb stood alone. It takes courage to stand alone. More than that, it takes character to stand alone—especially for a young person. It takes no character to smoke pot with the others—any coward can do that. It takes no character to drink with the rest of the crowd—any coward can do that. It takes no character to sleep around, but it does takes character to stand alone and refuse to be like everyone else.

I have discovered that kind of character is found more often in young people than in adults, and more often in women than in men. A willingness to stand alone in the faith when family and friends oppose you takes character.

Character Finishes Well

The thing that stands out most vividly about Caleb is not how he started, but how he finished. "As yet I am as strong this day as on the day that Moses sent me; just as my strength was then, so now is my strength for war, both for going out and for coming in" (v. 11).

Bear with me as I interpret this a bit differently from what most people would. If you read the commentaries on Joshua, you will note the remark about how healthy Caleb must have been to be as physically strong at 85 as he was at 45. But I suspect they are missing the point. When Caleb said, "I am as strong this day as on the day that Moses sent me," he was not just talking about his body. He was talking about his spirit as well.

An 85-year-old body cannot compare to a 40-year-old body. Caleb was aging, but part of him was being renewed daily. Not the outside, but the inside. Caleb finished well. His faith never failed—he held on.

This may be the greatest testimony we have. The way we start is not as important as how we finish. Many a person has started well; far fewer have finished so. The apostle Paul knew the importance of a good finish. Speaking to Timothy, he made the following statement:

> For I am already being poured out as a drink offering, and the time of my departure is at hand. I have fought the good fight, I have finished the race, I have kept the faith. Finally, there is laid up for me the crown of righteousness, which the Lord, the righteous Judge, will give me on that Day, and not to me only but also to all who have loved His appearing (2 Timothy 4:6-8).

You may have heard this story. In 1973, on a small island in the Philippines, a Japanese soldier was discovered. He had been hiding there since 1942. He did not know the war had ended. Thirty-one years had passed. When they asked him how he could hold out so long, he replied, "The last thing my commanding officer told me was, 'Hold on until I return.'"

In a sense, Jesus has said the same thing to all of us—"Hold on until I return." Character finishes well.

172

Discussion Questions

1. Why are people impressed with celebrities?

2. Paul implied that God does His work through people that the world considers to be nobodies. Why? What does this have to do with character?

3. Do you agree that people often stop living before they die?

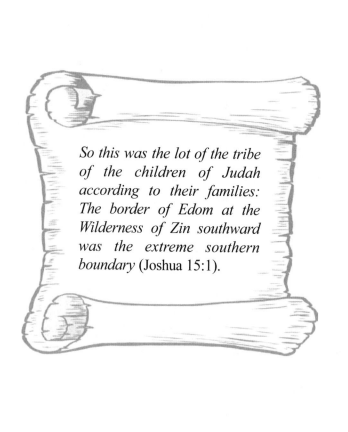

So this was the lot of the tribe of the children of Judah according to their families: The border of Edom at the Wilderness of Zin southward was the extreme southern boundary (Joshua 15:1).

15

The Blessed Life

How often have you prayed the prayer "Bless me, Lord"? A thousand times? Ten thousand? It is the most often uttered request. "God bless me. God bless my family. God bless my home. God bless the choir members tonight as they sing. God bless the church. God bless the worship service. God bless my children. God bless the food we are about to eat."

I have a question for you. In fact, I have three questions for you. If God blessed you, would you know it? If you knew it, could you handle it? If you knew it and you could handle it, would you share it? Promised-life people are blessed. However, the truth is, most of us do not understand the blessing.

Joshua 15—22 are difficult to read. I hope you don't think me irreverent for saying this, but "facts is facts." And the fact is, these are among the most mind-numbing, dull, tedious verses in the Bible. In them, Joshua lists the divisions of the land among the tribes. He describes borders and property boundaries. This is about as exciting to read as a voter registration list.

Incidentally, this is one of the reasons I believe the Bible is fact and not fiction. No writer of fiction in his right mind would have put in something as dull as these seven chapters. However, as difficult as they are to read, they do contain several dynamic truths, though we do have to dig deep to find them. I want to condense these chapters to three lessons concerning the blessings of God.

LESSON ONE: THE GREATER THE BLESSING, THE GREATER THE RESPONSIBILITY

To whom much is given, much is required. Clearly the blessing of God places tremendous responsibility upon us. "To whom much is given, from him much will be required; and to whom much has been committed, of him they will ask the more" (Luke 12:48).

This principle plays out beginning with Joshua 15. This is the account of the division of land to the tribe of Judah. In verses 20-63 is a list of all the villages and cities that were given to the tribe of Judah—98 cities in all. In other words, the tribe of Judah was blessed more than any other tribe. This one tribe was given almost the entire southern region of Canaan.

What a blessing! However, there was a catch. Judah was given more, but more would be asked of them than of any other tribe. To the south of Judah were the enemies of Israel, among them the Amalekites and the Philistines. When the other tribes were at peace in the land, Judah continued to fight. For years to come, they would serve as the buffer between the other tribes and their enemies.

176

There is nothing wrong with desiring the blessing of God, or even asking for more. However, do understand that God does not bless you just so you can be fat and happy. When God blesses, He does so for a purpose.

I think about our nation. In the history of the world there has never been a nation greater than ours. If you have never traveled outside this country, you may not be aware of how abundant this land really is. You have to see the rest of the world to appreciate what we have. So . . .

- Why should our nation be responsible for helping the needy of the world?

- Why should our tax money go to take care of people in other places?

- Why should we care about starving children in the Sudan or genocide in Rwanda?

- Why should we care about ethnic cleansing in the Balkans?

- Why should we care about a dictator who abuses his people and threatens the peace of his region?

Why? Because to whom much is given, much is required. And our nation has been given much.

I also think of how blessed you and I are. God has given us so much. Do not make the mistake of thinking you have all that you have because of your hard work. It is the Lord your God who gives you strength to gain your wealth. He has not only given you money—he has also given you talent, intelligence and opportunity. What blessings we have.

LESSON TWO: THE PASSIVE LIFE IS RARELY THE BLESSED LIFE

God does help those who help themselves. Joshua 16—17 describe two tribes sharing one parcel of land. These are called the children of Joseph, consisting of the tribes of Ephraim and Manasseh. In this account, the two tribes complain, because they do not have as much as the other tribes. "Then the children of Joseph spoke to Joshua, saying, 'Why have you given us only one lot and one share to inherit, since we are a great people, inasmuch as the Lord has blessed us until now?' " (17:14).

Ephraim and Manasseh, the sons of Joseph, complained to Joshua. To paraphrase, they said, "Joshua, we are not blessed enough. We do not have enough land. You have given just one share between us. We cannot raise our crops and graze our cattle on the small parcel of land allotted to us."

> So Joshua answered them, "If you are a great people, then go up to the forest country and clear a place for yourself there in the land of the Perizzites and the giants, since the mountains of Ephraim are too confined for you." But the children of Joseph said, "The mountain country is not enough for us; and all the Canaanites who dwell in the land of the valley have chariots of iron, both those who are of Beth Shean and its towns and those who are of the Valley of Jezreel." And Joshua spoke to the house of Joseph—to Ephraim and Manasseh—saying, "You are a great people and have great power; you shall not have only one lot, but the mountain country shall be yours. Although it is wooded, you shall cut it down, and its farthest extent shall be yours; for you shall drive out the Canaanites, though they have iron chariots and are strong" (vv. 15-18).

Let me paint the picture. These people did not think they were very blessed. They wanted more, and so Joshua replied, "If you want greater blessings from God, get up, take your axe, cut down the trees, take your sword, run off the Canaanites." In other words, "If you don't think you have enough, get up and do something about it." The picture is of people who sit around complaining, but do not help themselves.

The passive life is rarely ever the blessed life. God does help people who help themselves. I encounter so many who have a desire in their heart, but who never do anything about that desire. There is something they want in life, but they never pursue it.

For many, the problem is the "failure of fatalism." They assume there is no hope for anything better in life. Other people suffer from the "paralysis of analysis." They dream about what they want, but they do nothing about it.

Let me offer a word of advice. If you want more, do more. I do not know if your dream will ever be fulfilled or your desire ever achieved, but I do know this: If you do not go for it, you will never have it. The principle is simple: Passive lives are rarely blessed lives.

Have you always had a desire to be a college graduate? Well, do something about it. Start by taking one class. Someone might complain, "But I am 50 years old. If I go back to school, it will take me five years to complete it. I will be 55 years old by the time I graduate." So what? In five years you are going to be 55 whether you go to school or not. You could be 55 with your degree, or you can do nothing and be 55 without it. Passive lives are rarely ever blessed lives.

LESSON THREE: THE BLESSING YOU HAVE IS BIGGER THAN YOU THINK

Little is much when God is in it. As you read chapters 18—22, you will notice that Joshua begins to pick up speed. He no longer elaborates or comments on the divisions of the land. Instead, he simply lists the names and the properties given to them. Other than a passage concerning cities of refuge, there really is not much in these verses to get excited about, except for one passage of Scripture. In the midst of these mind-numbing details, Joshua mentions a tiny little tribe with a tiny little section of land.

> Now the lot of the tribe of the children of Benjamin came up according to their families, and the territory of their lot came out between the children of Judah and the children of Joseph (18:11).

This verse describes the division of the land to the tribe of Benjamin. The smallest of all tribes, they were given the smallest portion of the land. Benjamin had been given a little strip of territory between the lands of Judah and the lands of Ephraim and Manasseh.

It did not look like very much, but oh my, what God did with it and with its inhabitants! From that tiny strip of land came many of the greatest leaders in Israel's history: the greatest kings, judges, military leaders and prophets. From the prophet Jeremiah to the apostle Paul, greatness came out of that land.

When I read of the tribe of Benjamin, and I see all that God has done, I am reminded that so much can be done with so little when God is in it. We read of this throughout the Bible. Consider the story of David, not when he was a mighty king, but when he was just a boy. He faced Goliath without much to offer. I love the story. David put on the armor of Saul, but he could not handle it. He slumped beneath the weight of it and fell over. So, little David went out on his own, armed only with a strap of leather, a hand full of smooth stones and childlike faith. But little was much when God was in it.

We read the story of the little boy with the loaves and fishes. It was not much to offer—only the lunch his mother had prepared for him. It was not much, but oh my, what God did with it!

We read the story of the poor widow who had only a mite to throw in the offering. (A mite is the equivalent of one quarter of one penny.) This was not much to offer, but more money has come into the Kingdom because of that quarter of a cent than anything else I can think of. The blessings you have are bigger than you know, when you put them in God's hands.

Some of you may think you have little to offer God, but you do not know what God can do with it. I love Steven Brown's statement: "God loves you so much that if He had a wallet, your picture would be in it." But it is not just that He loves you—He can use you. It does not matter what you have to offer . . . little is much when God is in it.

I think of the Cross. The death of Christ on the cross was something few people knew about, and at the time, no one fully understood. To most observers, it was the death of an obscure man in an obscure place. In the scheme of human history, it seemed a relatively small thing, but that little thing has overcome the world.

My salvation was that way. It didn't look like much to anybody in that church that day, nor did it seem like much to me. But it changed my whole life. Little is much when God is in it. My, how God blesses! How He blesses indeed!

Discussion Questions

1. To whom much is given, much is required. How does this apply to you personally? What is required of you as a result of your unique blessing?

2. Though the statement "God helps those who help themselves" does not appear in the Bible, does it express a Biblical concept?

3. How do you explain the remarkable blessings that we in the United States enjoy, when so much of the rest of the world is in need?

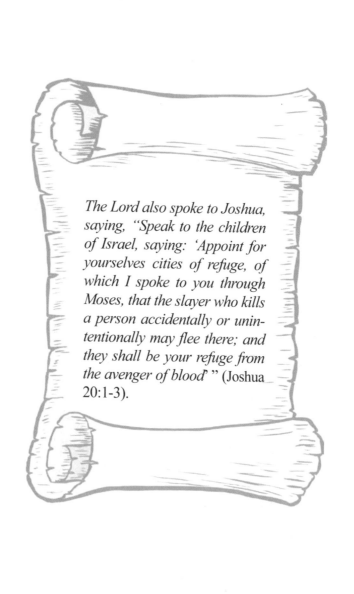

The Lord also spoke to Joshua, saying, "Speak to the children of Israel, saying: 'Appoint for yourselves cities of refuge, of which I spoke to you through Moses, that the slayer who kills a person accidentally or unintentionally may flee there; and they shall be your refuge from the avenger of blood'" (Joshua 20:1-3).

16

Eternal Ethics

Joshua 20:1-9

A re you an ethical person? I hope you are. No doubt you think you are. In fact, most people do. From where or what did you get your ethic? How did you form your value system? These questions may sound strange, but it is very important that you answer them thoughtfully. I suspect that most people form their ethic simply by observing the culture around them and adopting its values. These are what I call "good old boy" values. Good old boy values are easy to spot. They are summarized in statements like the following:

- "Do unto others before they get a chance to do it unto you."

- "I just believe in 'live and let live.' Don't bother anybody."

- "You only go around once; grab all the gusto you can get."

I came across a little rhyme called the "Redneck Ethic" that also expresses this value system. Although we wouldn't agree with its instruction, it lets us know how many people think.

Make the world a better place,
  Love one another.
Do your part for the human race,
  Share your beer with a brother.

I am not far off the mark when I say the source for most people's ethical enlightenment is television. Television may be the most effective tool ever devised to influence and shape people's values.

But what about the child of God—the believer? We are striving to live the promised life. To do so requires that we live by a different ethic. From what and where does the believer derive his value system? That is not hard to answer. Our values are to come from our faith. Our ethic is to be God's ethic. We are to hold valuable what He holds valuable. The question is, What is it that God holds valuable? Joshua 20 will help us see that.

This is a most unusual account. These verses form another parenthetic passage, an interruption to the main flow of the story. The children of Israel are in the process of settling into the land, dividing up the territory, and staking out their claims. As this is being done, Joshua issues a decree that six cities were to be set aside as cities of refuge.

A look at the background will be helpful at this point. This was a wild, wide-open time. It was not unlike our stereotype of the American Wild West, when vengeance was the order of the day. In the midst of this, Joshua realizes a problem. If he does not do something, vigilante law will rule. So Joshua established six cities of refuge to serve as places where people could go to be protected from vigilante justice until their case could be heard. For example, if a man killed another man, before vengeance could be taken against him, he could flee to one of the six cities of refuge to escape the avenger of blood, which was typically a family member of the slain man, who had been entrusted to exact revenge.

These six cities were stationed all around the country. By law, every region of the land was required to have at least one. Ideally, no person would live more than a day's walk from a city of refuge.

What value is this story to us? Some see no value in it; many commentaries simply mention it in passing without considering any of its merit. To the other extreme are those who see it as a "type" or analogy of Christ, who is our refuge. I believe there is more to this story. It is not recorded just as interesting historic filler. In this account, we learn something of the eternal ethic. From it, we can derive—at least in part—what God holds valuable.

Life

God values life. God holds life sacred; therefore, you and I ought to hold life sacred as well. This passage warns against the indiscriminate taking of life.

Why does God value life? Among other reasons, life is precious because it is so fragile. James says, "For what is your life? It is even a vapor that appears for a little time and then vanishes away" (4:14). The word *vapor* means "fog or mist." Fog looks substantial, but it really is not. I have seen the fragile nature of life and have learned much about it over the years. I have conducted funerals for a 20-year-old man who died of an unexpected heart attack, a 17-year-old boy murdered in a drive-by shooting, and a little girl born with a brain defect that took her life at the age of 4.

One of the most difficult occasions of my ministry

came as I held a man in my arms to keep him from col-lapsing as he held the limp body of his 2-year-old son. The boy had been with his father on a tractor when he fell and was crushed by the tires of the tractor. Life is fragile.

The things that are most fragile are typically the things we hold most valuable. You might throw an old pot or pan into a cabinet, but you would never toss your fragile china and porcelain around that way. Why? Because they are so fragile. Life is like that. Because it is so fragile, God holds it sacred, and so should we. The trouble is, we live in a culture that is rapidly devaluing life.

There is an axiom of truth that applies to us. The further a society moves away from the concept of an absolute God, the more that society will devalue human life. This is a simple but irrefutable truth. It does not require great powers of observation to see how much we have devalued human life in recent years. The evidence is pervasive.

1. *Abortion.* More than 1 million babies are put to death in their mother's womb every year, with a significant number of these in the third trimester of pregnancy. I know the argument; I have heard it many times. Some will say, "We must have abortion on demand because of extenuating circumstances such as rape, incest and the health of the mother." I would almost agree with that. In fact, I could almost support legislation that would allow abortion for those reasons. I said I could almost support it, and for this reason. Under that legislation, most abortions would end. The vast majority of abortions are per-formed for the sake of convenience.

2. *Euthanasia.* This is abortion's ugly stepsister. Thirty years ago, Christian ethicists argued against abortion, warning it would open the door to other horrifying possi-bilities. Abortion, they feared, would place us on a slippery

slope toward euthanasia of the elderly. The social engineers of the time laughed and characterized Christians as cultural buffoons. No one is laughing now. Today's ethical debate concerns euthanasia. This is not hard to understand. If we do not value life at its beginning, why would we value it at its end?

3. *Physician-assisted suicide.* This is a natural follow-through from euthanasia. If we have the right to take someone else's life when we no longer deem it to have quality, surely it logically follows that we should have the right to take our own, with the assistance of our kind family doctor of course.

4. *Racism.* This is an often overlooked evidence of the devaluing of human life. I do not believe a person can be a Christian and a bigot at the same time. I cannot see how the Spirit of Christ and the spirit of bigotry can coexist in a person. Racism is a perverted sense of value concerning human life. It holds that one life is inherently more important than another life. Nonsense. Not in God's eyes, and God's values are to be our values.

One other thing before we leave this point: God values your life. You matter to God, so much so that He sent His Son into the world to die for you. God values life.

Justice

God values justice. In fact, God values justice more than life. Life is sacred, but God will sacrifice life for the sake of justice. "And he shall dwell in that city until he stands before the congregation for judgment" (Joshua 20:6).

An accused man could dwell safely in a city of refuge, but not forever. One day he must be judged. God values justice. He is the God of righteousness, holiness and justice. If need be, He will sacrifice life so that justice may be served. Some people believe that capital punishment and Christian values are incongruent. Not so. There are some things for which only death will bring justice.

If God values justice, so should we. This involves more than legal restitution. It speaks to social justice as well. The Scripture repeatedly speaks of the right of the poor, the needy and the disenfranchised of the world.

Is there a reason we ought to be interested in equal rights for women? Certainly there is. Why? Because Jesus was interested in equal rights for women. Is there a reason why we ought to be interested in human rights for the disenfranchised poor around the world? Of course. Jesus was interested in human rights for the disenfranchised poor. Should we be concerned for the civil rights of minorities? Yes, because Jesus was. God values justice. We ought to value justice as well.

Mercy

God values mercy. In fact, God values mercy above all. God values life, but He values justice more than life. God values justice, but He values mercy more than justice. He will suspend justice for the sake of mercy. There is an interesting statement in Joshua 20. I am probably making more of it than I should, but it seems to be very significant. "These were the cities appointed for all the children of Israel and for the stranger who dwelt among them" (v. 9). The key phrase is "the stranger who dwelt among them." Who are these strangers? These are the Canaanites. You must keep in mind that God had been judging the Canaanites. Joshua had been told to destroy them all. But when we get to the end of the conquest, we find the Lord extending mercy to the Canaanites, provided they seek it. If they come to a city of refuge, they are to be given refuge.

There is a principle here: Anyone who seeks refuge with God finds mercy in God. God values mercy over justice, and He will suspend justice in order to give mercy. The New Testament corollary is stated like this: "Whoever calls on the name of the Lord shall be saved" (Acts 2:21; Romans 10:13). "Whosoever will come . . . let him . . ." (Mark 8:34, KJV).

Have you noticed that religious people do not seem to value mercy as much as they do law? There is a great account in the New Testament of an encounter between Jesus and a prostitute. She fell at His feet, washed them with her tears, and dried them with her hair. Then she kissed His feet and anointed them with fragrant oil. The indignant religious crowd took offense to such improper behavior. But Jesus said, "Her sins, which are many, are forgiven" (see Luke 7:36-48). How unlike so many churches today.

Does your church have the reputation of being a "grace place"—a place where "whosoever will [may] come?" Is it the kind of place where people, whose lives are in a mess, can find help? Is it a place where sinners are welcome and grace is freely given? If your church is not a grace place, it is not a church. It is just a religious fraternity.

I had been preaching in a very aristocratic Southern town. The pastor had asked me to spend the entire weekend preaching on marriage and family. It was the last service I was to preach. Things had gone well the first two nights. The choir was preparing to sing just before I was to speak. I noticed a buzz in the congregation. People in the choir were leaning over, talking to one another, and pointing to the back of the sanctuary. Coming through the doors of the church was a young, but haggard-looking, woman. Everyone seemed to know her. I leaned over to the pastor, who was sitting next to me, and asked, "Who is that young woman? What is her story?"

"Oh," he said, "she is a prostitute."

I said, "Really." It was a small town, and prostitutes were not an everyday sight. The pastor went on to explain, "She is actually a relative of a church member. She moved to a larger city and was arrested for prostitution, and everyone knows it. But she has come back home to our town." I wondered how this sort of person would be received in such an aristocratic church, so I watched for a few moments as she just stood at the door—uncertain and hesitant.

At that moment I saw an amazing thing happen. One of the most proper Southern women you could imagine got up, walked over to the young prostitute, hugged her, and said, "Please come sit with me."

When the service concluded, the young woman asked to speak to me alone. This young prostitute and I went back to the pastor's office where she told me the story of how she got started in prostitution. Then she said, "I don't want that life anymore." I began to talk to her of Christ and His promise to give her a new life. I concluded by telling her that she could at that very moment receive Him as Lord of her life. I offered to help her pray. Immediately, she knelt, and I knelt beside her. That night as we prayed together the sinner's prayer, the young prostitute gave her heart to Christ. I believe when she began the prayer she was a prostitute; but by the time she ended her prayer, she had become a child of the King. Mercy drops were falling in that place. That is what God holds dear. God values mercy and so should you.

Discussion Questions

1. To what extent has television shaped your value system, as opposed to your children's value system?

2. Do you agree that Christians should get involved with issues of social justice? If so, to what extent?

3. Can we differentiate between the mercy of God and the grace of God?

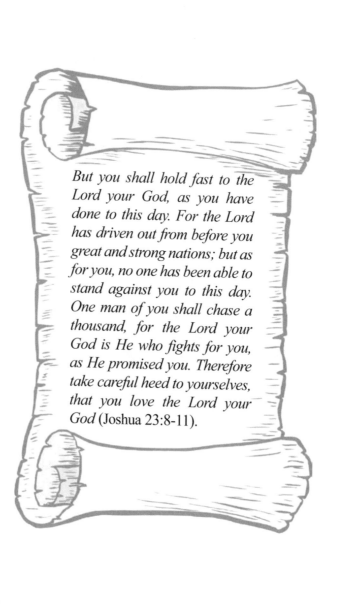

But you shall hold fast to the Lord your God, as you have done to this day. For the Lord has driven out from before you great and strong nations; but as for you, no one has been able to stand against you to this day. One man of you shall chase a thousand, for the Lord your God is He who fights for you, as He promised you. Therefore take careful heed to yourselves, that you love the Lord your God (Joshua 23:8-11).

17

God Is in Charge

Joshua 23

I turned on the radio just in time. The question was being asked of one of America's leading theologians: "What is the most important truth you know about God?" His answer was classic: "The most important truth I know about God is that there is a God and I'm not Him." Isn't that great? There is a God, and I am not Him. That says it all.

In case you didn't get it, let me paraphrase: "Somebody else is in charge, not me. All I have to do is stay on His side." That is the greatest truth any of us can know. Joshua knew this as well. As we begin the 23rd chapter, Joshua is an old man, and he knows that he will soon die. "Now it came to pass, a long time after the Lord had given rest to Israel from all their enemies round about, that Joshua was old, advanced in age" (v. 1).

When I say Joshua was an old man, I mean he was a very old man—110 years old.

I have liked Joshua at every stage of his life. I liked him when he was a young man full of vim, vigor and vitality, ready to take on the world. I liked him when he was a mature man and God used him to lead the children of Israel out of the wilderness and into the Promised Land. But I especially like Joshua, the old guy. I really do. He's an old guy with a really great attitude. Not all old people have great attitudes, but Joshua did.

When I first began in ministry, someone told me the three things to always remember: every bride is beautiful, every baby is sweet, and every old person is lovable. After 30 years in ministry, I have discovered that none of these are universally true. I have seen some ugly brides, I've been around some horrendous kids, and I've known some miserable, sour, bitter, old people. But Joshua was an old man with a great attitude. He had aged with style and grace. That is the way we all should age, but is not easy to do. Growing old can be a bum deal.

As we grow old, the body begins to fail. An elderly man told me that he felt like a young man trapped in an old man's body. I am beginning to understand more and more what that means.

Not only does the body begin to fail; the mind begins to fog. That is why some of you think the "good old days" were good.

Not only does the mind fog, and the body fail, but looks begin to fade as well. There is a certain point in time when we will not look the way we look now. It will get worse. It is hard to age with grace and style, but Joshua did.

This graceful old man has now come to the point in his life when he knows he is going to die soon. Knowing he is not long for this world, he wants to leave some word for his loved ones to live by. Beginning with verse 3, he distills the wisdom of 110 years into this one passage. All that he says can be summarized like this: "God is in charge, stay on His side." "For the Lord your God is He who has fought for you" (v. 3).

In other words, all the victories you have enjoyed are the result of God's intervention. All this, while you thought you did it. But it was not you—it was the Lord your God who fought for you. Verse 10 adds, "One man of you shall chase a thousand, for the Lord your God is He who fights for you."

The idea is this: You might think you are chasing the enemy out of the land, but it is God doing it. You thought you were winning the land, but it was God who did that. It is God who fought for you. It is God who fights for you now. It is God who will fight for you in the future. He is in charge. Therefore, love the Lord your God. Just stay on His side. How does this apply?

The Big Picture

Get the big picture. God is in charge of the world. The whole thing is in His hands. Understand that, and relax a little bit. Just make sure you are on His side. At times it may look as though He is not in charge. When you look around at all the things that are happening, you may wonder, *Where is God in all of this?* In recent years, we have witnessed incredible and disturbing things taking place. Our nation was victimized by the worst terrorism attack in history. We have gone to war in two nations—Afghanistan and Iraq. We have experienced one of the largest stock market plunges in our history, probably second only to the Great Depression. Unemployment has gone up, finances are a problem everywhere, charities are going out of business, and churches are suffering shortfalls.

We are being warned of new viruses that are taking

hold. The SARS virus, we are told, could become pandemic—causing the deaths of thousands of people. We wonder, *Where is God? Is God really in charge?* But then we come back to Joshua and read, "It is the Lord your God who is fighting for you." It is the Lord your God who is in charge. If you do not know this, you will never understand how life works. In fact, you will never be able to understand history if you do not know that God is in charge of it.

As I see it, there are four ways of looking at history. The first is sometimes called the *evolutionist perspective* of history. The evolutionist says that all of history is a cause-and-effect sequence of events. In other words, one thing is causing the next thing, and humanity is moving onward and upward.

Then there is the *fatalist view* of history, which sees life as a cycle of issues that continue to repeat. There are different faces, different names, but the same issues over and over again.

Then, for lack of better way of saying it, there is what I sometimes called the *postmodern perspective* of history. This is the idea that history means nothing. It is going nowhere, consisting of one random event after another.

We can summarize these philosophies with these three statements: The evolutionist believes one thing leads to another, the fatalist believes what goes around comes around, and the postmodernist believes stuff just happens.

But there is a fourth view of history—the *eternal view*. The eternal view says that history did not just begin; God began it. History is not going to just end; God is going to end it. God is in charge of everything from its beginning to its end. That is the eternal view. This is what Joshua wanted the children of Israel to know. All that they had gone through, God was in it; and all you go through, God is in it.

For me this is remarkably "un-stressing." One of the most liberating truths I know is that God is in charge, not me. There have been times when I thought I was. I knew the world functioned well before I got here, but I wasn't quite certain it could function if I left.

Here is a liberating truth. You are not that important. Neither am I. In the eternal scheme of things, we are relatively minor players. God is in charge of it all. That takes a tremendous weight off my shoulders. I do not have to carry the weight of the world around, because God is in charge. Relax, just stay on His side.

A Personal Reality

We have looked at the general application. What about the personal dimension? What Joshua wanted the people to know is not just that God is in charge of *the* world; he wanted them to understand that God is in charge of *their* world. Joshua believed that God was in control of his individual life.

There is not one thing you have ever been through that God was not in. There is not one thing you are going through that God is not in. And there is not one thing you will go through that God will not be in. God is in charge.

I do not mean to suggest that everything that happens to you is God-ordained. I am simply saying that in everything that happens to you, God is in charge. God takes charge of everything. This is another great truth that, when properly understood, will set you free.

There was a time when I thought I was in charge of my life. I thought the only way things would work out was if I *made* them work out. Then I discovered this truth: God is in charge of my life—all of my life. I may not be a major player in the scheme of God, but I am a major concern to the heart of God. God is in charge of my life and yours.

As I look back at my life, I can see so many things God had to be in charge of or they would never have worked out. Throughout my childhood, there were so many things God was controlling. Then into my youth and adulthood, God clearly was at work.

After high school, I went to college and promptly flunked out. Notice I said *flunked out*, not *dropped out*. Do you know the difference between dropping out and flunking out? *Dropping out* is your idea; *flunking out* is the school's idea. I was out of college for three years. I thought it was a terrible thing. But during those three years, God was in charge. He used that time to change my life dramatically.

At that time I had a job I thought would last, but then I got fired. I thought this was a disastrous turn of events, but God was in charge. As a result of getting fired, I was motivated to return to college. It took some begging, but I was allowed back in on probation. After three years, I was ready and able to learn. I have often assumed God was not in my circumstance, only to find out He was *always* in charge.

I can look at my years in ministry and can see how God has been in charge. I have had successes, and I have known failure. I have climbed, and I have fallen. I have gone up, and I have gone down. I have done things well, and I have made some colossal mistakes. I did not always know it at the time, but in every one of those occasions, God was in charge and knew exactly what He was doing. I believe that God was in charge on the day I was born and before, and He is going to be in charge the day I die and beyond.

C.S. Lewis wrote a book titled *Letters to an American Lady*, a compilation of letters. In one, he writes to a woman he calls Mary. He has learned that Mary has terminal cancer, and the doctors had stopped her treatments. He writes:

Dear Mary,

This is terrible news. The doctor who refused treatment to you would be liable for prosecution in my country. Pain is a terrible thing, but truly you need not have fear as well. Can you not see, Mary, that death is a friend? It means slipping off the body which has tormented you for so long. What is there to be afraid of? You have long lived the Christian life and your sins are forgiven. Has this world been so kind that you would leave it with such regret, Mary? There are better things ahead than there are behind.

Are you struggling? Are you resisting? Don't you think our Lord would say, "Mary, be at peace. Child, let go. Underneath you are the everlasting arms. Let go, Mary, I will catch you."

I am yours and like you, a tired traveler near the end of his journey.

How could Lewis write such a letter? He knew God was in charge. From the moment you are born and before, until the moment you die and beyond, God is in charge. Are you having financial problems? God is in charge. Has a loved one died? God is in charge. Do you have cancer?

God is in charge. Has your whole life been turned upside down? God is in charge. All you have to do is "love the Lord your God" (Mark 12:30). Stay on His side.

September 11, 2001, is a date that I doubt any of us will ever forget. I remember exactly where I was and the details of the entire day. I remember the moment I was told that the World Trade Center towers had been struck. I remember every appointment I had that day and every person with whom I talked. That day is emblazoned on my memory. I will never forget Tuesday, September 11, 2001.

Almost as vivid in my mind is what happened the next day—the evening of September 12. It was a Wednesday night, the first time the church had gathered since the tragedy. The sanctuary was packed. I was uncertain what to do. I did not know if I should preach or pray. As I walked in, the sanctuary was silent. You could have heard the proverbial pin drop—it was that quiet. People were kneeling at the altar in prayer. Those in the pews sat with heads bowed, and some were crying. The lights had been dimmed. There was no conversation. All that was heard was the whisper of people praying.

When time came, I stepped to the platform, still not certain what to do. For a moment I simply stood there and stared at them. Then, reverently and softly, I began singing. As I did, one person joined in, and then another person began to sing as well, and then another and another. Then everyone stood to their feet, and sang over and over, louder and louder:

> He's got the whole world in His hands.
> He's got the whole wide world in His hands.
> He's got the whole world in His hands.
> He's got the whole world in His hands.

Indeed He does have the whole world in His hands, and He has your world in His hands as well. God is in charge. Stay on His side.

Discussion Questions

1. If God is in charge of all things, does that mean everything that happens is ordained by God?

2. Does God take sides in world events? Is it right to ask Him to be on our side?

3. If God is involved in every aspect of my life, to what extent am I responsible for the way it turns out?

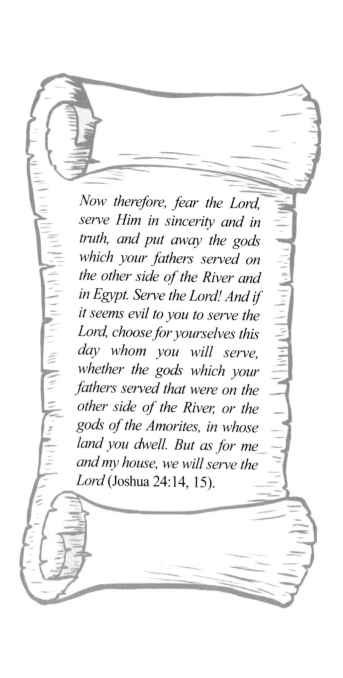

Now therefore, fear the Lord, serve Him in sincerity and in truth, and put away the gods which your fathers served on the other side of the River and in Egypt. Serve the Lord! And if it seems evil to you to serve the Lord, choose for yourselves this day whom you will serve, whether the gods which your fathers served that were on the other side of the River, or the gods of the Amorites, in whose land you dwell. But as for me and my house, we will serve the Lord (Joshua 24:14, 15).

18

Make Up Your Mind

Joshua 24

Life is filled with choices. From the moment you get up in the morning, to the moment you go to bed at night, you have decisions to make. Not every choice matters greatly. Your choice to eat oatmeal rather than bran flakes for breakfast is not that significant. On the other hand, some choices are absolutely crucial: what you will do in life, where you will live, whom you will marry, are all choices that matter. They are crucial choices to make.

Sartre, the French philosopher, said, "[You make your choices], and it is through these choices and living that man defines who and what he is." The longer you live, the more you will realize how true this is. You are where you are in life largely because of the choices you made in the past.

Of all the choices we make in life, the most critical choice is not where we will live, what we will do, or whom we will marry. The most critical choice in life is this: Will my life count for God?

In this 24th and final chapter, Joshua realizes his time

is at hand. As the apostle Paul would later write in the New Testament about his own life, Joshua has run his race and has finished his course (see 2 Timothy 4:7). He realizes that he is not long for this world. But before he dies, he wants to do all he can to secure the future of his people. They have settled the land. Almost everything has been accomplished, but there is one thing left to do. They must make a choice concerning their future. You will not understand this passage of Scripture until you know something of the context.

In verses 1-13, Joshua has described the good hand of God upon those who love Him, those who are faithful to Him. Beginning with verse 19 through the end of the chapter, he talks about the heavy hand of God against those who have not chosen for Him—those who are not faithful to Him. But right in the middle of these two things, Joshua calls the people to make a choice. What will it be? Will you know the blessing of God on the faithful, or will you know the heavy hand of God on the unfaithful? The choice is yours.

A Personal Choice

The choice is personal; it is an individual decision that no one can make for you. "And if it seems evil to you to serve the Lord, choose for yourselves" (v. 15).

This is a choice that every person and every generation must make. Note the generational dynamic at play in this passage. Remember that Joshua, 110 years old, is worn out. Life had been hard, long and difficult. Joshua is not only an old man, he is the last of his generation. He is looking now at a younger generation to carry forth, but they must choose for themselves.

Joshua has reminded them that their forefathers had made up their minds, and now it was their turn. Every generation must decide. In essence he was saying, "You have to make up your own mind now. What your forefathers decided in the past does not matter. It is your time to stand and be counted."

There is no "righteousness by inheritance." Some people seem to think that if their father was a Christian, their grandfather was a Christian and their great-grandfather was a Christian that somehow, through a process of osmosis, they are Christian too. As the old saying goes, "Just because you are born in a bakery does not necessarily make you a doughnut." Likewise, if you were born to a Christian family, that does not make you a Christian. Thank God for your heritage, but it counts for nothing between you and God. There is a choice, and you must make it. There is no righteousness by inheritance.

There is no "salvation by association." You are not saved because you know saved people. Men, I find, are particularly bad about this—especially as it concerns their wives. Men often marry above themselves spiritually. They like to marry good women. Some seem to think that if they marry a good woman, it will count for something with God. Sorry, guys, it does not work that way. Choose you this day for yourselves.

A Serious Choice

This decision is not one to be taken lightly. Unfortunately, many people do. In verse 15, Joshua exhorts the people to make up their mind. But beginning with verse 18, he seems to go ballistic with them when they do.

"And the Lord drove out from before us all the people, including the Amorites who dwelt in the land. We also will serve the Lord, for He is our God." But Joshua said to the people, "You cannot serve the Lord, for He is a holy God. He is a jealous God; He will not forgive your transgressions nor your sins. If you forsake the Lord and serve foreign gods, then He will turn and do you harm and consume you, after He has done you good" (vv. 18-20).

Whoa. Back up. Do you understand what has just happened? Joshua said, "Choose you this day whom you will serve." The people responded affirmatively, saying, "We will serve the Lord." Wonderful. You would think Joshua would be beside himself with joy. But instead of praising them, he says, "You are not going to truly serve the Lord. I warn you if you say you are and you don't follow through, God will consume you like a consuming fire."

Joshua was saying, "If you say you will follow the Lord, you had better mean business. This is a serious decision; don't take it lightly." To understand this reaction, we must get inside Joshua's head. Joshua was thinking the people had made a choice they had not thought through carefully.

This is a serious choice. It could be called an exclusive choice. Once you make it, you must exclude other things. There are certain things that are mutually exclusive in life. For example, you cannot be a law-abiding citizen and commit crime—those things are mutually exclusive. You cannot marry and live the single life—those things are mutually exclusive. You cannot call yourself a believer, a follower of Christ, and live like the rest of the world. But so often this is exactly what people do. That is why Joshua says what he does in verse 23. "Now therefore . . . put away the foreign gods which are among you, and incline your heart to the Lord God of Israel."

Evidently, during the conquest of Canaan, the people were gathering idols of foreign gods. Joshua said, "If you mean business, it is all or nothing. Get all that stuff out of your life."

So often the problem is that we make faith decisions, but we have not thought them through. Consequently, we do not really mean business by them. Churches are filled with people who made a decision, but never really meant anything by it. Monday through Saturday their lives do not count at all for the Kingdom, but they show up on Sunday for "church."

That is the point Joshua is making. "If you are going to serve the Lord, then go all the way. And if you are not going to follow all the way, then do not follow at all." Isn't that what Jesus said in the Revelation? "You are neither hot nor cold. I would rather you be hot than cold, be one or the other" (see 3:15, 16). This is a serious choice.

A Constant Choice

It is not only a personal choice and a serious choice, it is also a choice you must make over and over again. We tend to describe it as a once-in-a-lifetime, burn-all-the-bridges, choice. Let me tell you what it really is. It is a once-in-a-lifetime decision that you must make every day of your life. It is a once-in-a-lifetime decision, but every morning you must get up and choose again.

This is neither the first nor the last time these people have been asked to choose for the Lord. Moses, coming off the mountaintop, made them choose. He said, "Who will be on the Lord's side?" Just before they crossed the

Jordan, they had to choose whether or not they were going to do things God's way. After they conquered Jericho and Ai, they went to the valley of Shechem, where Joshua said, "OK, make up your mind; which way is it going to be?"

There are at least five occasions in the Book of Joshua when this choice is given in one form or another, and the choice will be put before them time and again in the future. Jeremiah will call them to make this choice. Elijah will call them to decide. Malachi will call them to choose.

I made the choice the summer of my 18th year. At the time, I considered it to be a once-in-a-lifetime decision. I would live my life for the Lord. But I make this same choice every day of my life. Every day I must ask the question, "Will I live for Him today or not?" At times, it is not day-by-day; rather, it is a moment-by-moment decision. When you find yourself in situations of moral temptation, you must decide at that moment, "Will I live for the Lord this moment or not?" Though you have made your decision long ago, there are times when you must say, "Lord, I am choosing You again."

Leighton Ford tells the story of a man in a testimony meeting, testifying about how God had blessed his life. He told how he was now a very wealthy man, but there was a time in his life when he had only $2 to his name. He said, "I came to church and heard the preacher give an appeal for missions. When I heard that appeal, my heart was moved, and I gave my last $2—all that I had—to the Lord." Then he smiled and said, "The rest is history. Now I am worth millions of dollars." As he sat back down, an elderly lady sitting in the pew behind him leaned over and whispered in a stage whisper for everyone to hear, "I dare you to do it again." It is a constant choice.

An Urgent Choice

Not only is it a personal choice, a serious choice and a constant choice, it is an urgent choice as well. Please note what Joshua says. "If it seems evil to you to serve the Lord, then choose you [watch this statement] this day." This expresses a sense of urgency. Joshua did not say, "You guys really ought to think about this. Let's give it a week or two and get together and see how you feel." No, he said, "Here are your choices. You are either going to live your life for God or not. You are either going to live for something greater than yourselves or, like everybody else, just live for yourselves. Make up your mind."

Do you know why it is so urgent? First, because life is brief. It goes by so fast. I don't know where all the time has gone. Yesterday, I looked young; today I do not. We hear this all the time; so often it seems trite and corny. But as my dad used to say, "Son, time flies." I would hear him say that and say, "Yeah, yeah, I know." But all the while I was thinking, *I have all the time in the world.* I do not think that way anymore. Where did the time go?

Psalm 90:5 speaks of your life as being a dream that passes. Have you ever had one of those dreams that seemed to last all night long? Experts tell us that the longest dreams last only a few seconds. Your life is much like that. It goes by so quickly. It seems like yesterday when I brought my firstborn son home. Now, he is married, and my two other children are now grown and out on their own. Where did the time go? Life is short.

Second, life is uncertain. You just never know what will happen next. That is why Joshua said, "Choose you this day." Life has a way of getting away from you before you know it.

So make up your mind. The promised life depends on it. As for me and my house, we have all chosen—we will serve the Lord. That is not the end of the matter; it is only the beginning.

Discussion Questions

1. How has your parents' faith affected your spiritual choices?

2. Explain the statement "Your decision for Christ is a once-in-a-lifetime choice that you must make every day of your life."

3. How is choosing to live for Christ an exclusive choice? How has it affected you in this regard?